FOLLOW THE GOLDEN BRICK ROAD

THE ULTIMATE PATH TO REAL ESTATE WEALTH BUILDING, RETIREMENT INCOME, AND FINANCIAL FREEDOM

ADVANCE PRAISE FOR FOLLOW THE GOLDEN BRICK ROAD

Fred is very professional, attentive to detail, and very easy to work with. Fred is a straight shooter and extremely honest. The process was incredibly easy and he was very responsive and thorough. I can recommend him to anyone seeking a professional Realtor.

Mike Bierman
MJCH LLC

Great book. The author, Fred Tichauer, has been instrumental in locating and negotiating contracts for houses which I have purchased for 38 years. His depth of real estate knowledge is exceptional; he is an expert in both residential and investment properties. His assessment of property value is factual and deliberate. Fred shares his knowledge, insight, and experience in this book. Reading it will serve you well in the real estate field.

Dr. Joe L. Davis
Professor Emeritus, University of Nebraska–Omaha

After retiring from the National Football League, I wanted to find a way to make money without being stuck behind a desk. I was always interested in real estate but had no experience prior to being introduced to Fred Tichauer. Not only did Fred walk me through every step of buying and holding real estate, but we built a genuine friendship along the way. He doesn't just talk a big game, he lives it, being an investor himself. I never thought I'd be able to expand my financial portfolio to this extent so quickly. Having the best mentor along with hard work, and here I stand corrected. Fred Tichauer, second to none!

Kenny Onatolu
Retired Linebacker, National Football League

I always wanted to own real estate but did not know how to get started. I met Fred Tichauer 13 years ago. Fred listened to my needs and wants, and he helped me understand that the best investment opportunities were with single-family homes. He taught me how to buy foreclosed properties with little to no money down, and he provided me with the resources and ongoing support to be successful. The first couple of properties were a learning experience, but once I figured out the system, I was able to rapidly grow my portfolio. I had many growth spurts where I doubled my portfolio size, and Fred supported me and provided guidance along the way. Today, I own 23 single-family homes with equity over 1 million dollars. There is no way I would ever be able to create a business with that kind of value with a limited investment. Fred taught me how to leverage my strong financial situation and use that to purchase real estate. Fred is also one of my closest friends, so not only did he help me become a millionaire, but I have a great friend for life. Thanks, Fred, for being my mentor!

Scott Simon
Simon Holdings LLC

As we were purchasing rental properties through our Self Directed 401k, finding someone like Fred was key to our success. Fred understood the intricacies of using 401k monies to purchase rentals as an investment and how it was different from purchasing properties with post-tax monies. Fred went above and beyond in supporting and guiding us through two trips to Omaha and multiple home purchases and securing an excellent property manager. Even after the purchases were made, he continues to check in with us to see how our investments are going. Working with Fred is the best first step any real estate investor could make!

Vaughn Hollingsworth
Travel Designer / Franchise Owner
Cruise Planners

Fred is one of the most influential people I have ever met in my life. I was lucky to have met Fred five years ago. Since that time he has guided me step-by-step through many real estate transactions with everyone having a different obstacle to overcome. He has showed me how to methodically build a steady stream of passive income through investing in single-family homes. This has provided my family and I true financial freedom. I never thought I could consider retiring before 40, but now it is a very realistic goal. Fred will always be someone I look up to for his strong work ethic, honesty, and true passion for helping people like me achieve their dreams.

Andy Terry
External Wholesaler
Ameritas

We are on our way to financial freedom because of Fred! Fred's knowledge and guidance have been instrumental to starting and developing our future in real estate investing. Over the past year, Fred has guided us through every step of the process of turning run-down houses into beautiful rental homes that create instant cash-flow machines. We have sincerely enjoyed getting to know Fred and working with him, and we are beyond grateful for his professionalism, expertise, and commitment to our success. Every step of the way, he has been there for us and goes above and beyond to provide us with the tools, resources, and support to be successful. We can't say enough about Fred's extensive knowledge and experience, passion for real estate investing, and dedication to his clients. We consider Fred to be a mentor and friend and are so thankful for all he has done for us on this incredible real estate journey!

Chris and Lavin Haberling

Fred Tichauer has been indispensable in growing our portfolio over the past 10 years. His approach to serving his clients by using an investor's mindset when analyzing opportunities has helped us navigate difficult markets, saving us an untold amount of hours and money.

Jason Bogner
Rolls Properties LLC

Fred's help was invaluable in getting us started with our rental houses. He was quick to steer us away from houses that had problems we would have overlooked, and recommended things we could do to increase the value of the properties we purchased.

Jim and Lynda Madison

I have had the opportunity to work with Fred for nearly 17 years. Over that period he has been both an asset and an inspiration. To date, I have bought and sold in excess of 180 homes and acquired a respectable rental portfolio. We may have disagreed from time to time on a project; however, Fred's desire to see those around him succeed has always shone through. His need to share his knowledge of this changing industry is truly selfless. I wish Fred all the success in the world on his crusade to broaden others' knowledge and abilities by sharing his insight and time.

Doug Riddington
K. R. Prop. LLC
DJTL Prop. LLC

FOLLOW THE GOLDEN BRICK ROAD

THE ULTIMATE PATH TO REAL ESTATE WEALTH BUILDING, RETIREMENT INCOME, AND FINANCIAL FREEDOM

FRED TICHAUER

Omaha, Nebraska

www.FredTichauer.com

First Edition: July 2019

Paperback: 978-0-9961382-7-7
Mobi: 978-0-9961382-8-4
EPUB: 978-0-9961382-9-1

Library of Congress Data on file with the publisher.

Printed in the United States of America.

10 9 8 7 6 5 4 3 2 1

This book is dedicated to the memory of my parents,
Walter and Helena Tichauer,
my children, Kelly, Randi, and Ryan,
and my grandchildren, Lauren, Emily, Jacob, Bayla,
Avigail, Esther, Yakov, and Quinn.

CONTENTS

FOREWORD

No matter whether you have an MBA, BA, two-year college degree, or high school diploma, don't ever let anyone tell you that you can't achieve financial freedom. Not only is it possible, it is much easier than you think. If you're willing to pay the price now, you will be rewarded later.

> *You gain strength, courage and confidence by every experience in which you really stop to look fear in the face... You must do the thing you think you cannot do.*
>
> —Eleanor Roosevelt

INTRODUCTION

As I started to think what I could cover in this book that hadn't already been said in thousands of books written about the real estate investment niche market, it became evident that the task was not going to be easy.

What should I include, what should I leave out, what is important to know, and what is nice to know?

In this book you are not going to find theories or far-fetched schemes for investing in real estate. Instead, I'll share practical knowledge and proven ideas that have worked for me for more than forty-five years as an investor.

I will get this out right now: There are no secrets about investing in real estate that anyone should pay tens of thousands of dollars for. Real estate investing is not rocket science or brain surgery. Rather than spending large amounts of money on a course taught by a self-proclaimed expert, you would be much better off using your hard-earned funds for a down payment or fix-up costs on a property.

The most important secret of success is finding a real estate agent in your community who is considered a residential investment specialist, is a landlord, has flipped properties, and understands your local market. When you find this person, you will be much closer to your destination than you could get by taking a seminar taught by someone who comes into town for one day and pretends to be an expert.

As your buyer agent, your local real estate investment specialist will be able to help you every step of the way. Best of all, getting this person's help will not cost you a cent.

Taking this path makes a lot more sense than purchasing high-priced systems or books that you'll end up selling on eBay. Many of those programs sound good on paper but in the end are nothing more than empty promises. Few investors will succeed by using them.

Bottom line: If you have good credit, access to money, and a solid financial statement, you can build wealth and ensure a comfortable retirement income. I can't think of any other business venture that will pay off this well if you take care of business. Again, your key is finding that knowledgeable agent, and better yet it won't cost you a dime if you are using that person as your buyer's agent.

Keep in mind that real estate is not complicated. Housing will always be a necessity for everyone, so as a business model it is a winner. Investing in residential real estate comes down to five key steps:

1. Find properties
2. Analyze properties
3. Buy properties
4. Fix properties
5. Sell or rent properties

We will cover these five steps in detail in Chapter 8.

Yes, real estate is the ticket to wealth building and retirement income. Even in the worst circumstances, it is impossible to lose all your money in this type of business. By contrast, maybe you have met people who lost all their money in the stock market or by opening their own business such as a pizza restaurant or bar. In later chapters I will explain why a real estate investment business is just about foolproof compared with a traditional small business.

More and more people are investing their hard-earned money in real estate instead of the stock market. As a matter of fact, real estate is now the number one investment option five years in the running. Real estate has met the test of time, and a lot of money is being made in this space.

I also believe in only buying properties that are worth owning, and that means they should be located in family-friendly neighborhoods. You will never go wrong if you take into consideration such things as a low crime rate, good schools, a park nearby, and easy access to a grocery, restaurants, and other necessities.

Why would anyone want to invest their hard-earned money in properties located in high-crime areas? Who will be the likely renter or buyer when it is time to sell? The property is not the problem; the neighborhood is the problem and you have to think about the type of tenants you want to attract. Most people, especially if they have children, want to rent the safest possible neighborhood.

There are lots of ways to make money in this business (wholesaling, lease options, rent-to-own, flipping, tax certificates, and more. If you plan on doing this for the long term, you need to think about the image you want to maintain in your community.

On any given day there are many properties available on the MLS. The most important question you need to ask yourself is whether you want to be known as an owner who takes pride in their properties and is a good neighbor who cares about improving the neighborhood or as someone who buys dumps, lets them deteriorate, and rents them to the first person who has the cash because they are only concerned about cash flow.

Over the years I have seen both types of property owners but fortunately very few so-called slum lords. Most investors keep their end goal in mind and only buy properties that are worth owning and will ultimately provide retirement income, wealth-building, and financial freedom.

I am often asked why I have only invested in houses, duplexes, and small apartments of six units or less, and my answer is that my comfort zone has always been houses. When it is time to execute your exit plan, who will be the likely buyer of a commercial property or a large apartment? It will be another investor, and trying to get investors to agree on what a property is worth will be like pulling teeth—very painful. On the other hand, a house is much easier to sell, and the likely buyer could be a first-time homeowner.

There is a lot of money to be made in this business, and your challenge is to decide where and how you want to proceed.

My background in real estate investment

I have a college degree, but it has nothing to do with real estate. I graduated from the University of Nebraska at Omaha in 1973 with a BS (you know what BS stand for) in Education and nobody has ever asked me what my major or grade point average was.

I started investing in real estate at age 21 when I purchased a duplex, moved into one side, and rented out the other. I thought it was a cool concept to have somebody else covering most of my monthly mortgage payment. When I sold the duplex three years later, I made enough money to make a down payment on three properties.

At that point, I decided that it might be a good idea to get a license, so in 1980 I enrolled in real estate classes. After failing the test twice, I finally passed on the third try and used my license solely to find, buy, and sell my own investment properties while working full-time as an executive with the Boy Scouts of America.

After a successful 24-year career with the BSA, I decided to try the free enterprise system and expand my real estate holdings. I had always thought that being independent of the workplace and taking charge of my own financial future was an appealing option. In 1998 I began a new career as a full-time real estate agent. I am considered an independent contractor. When people ask me who I work for, my response is that I work for myself and utilize the resources of the real estate company similar to way a franchise owner would use them in their business. Additionally, the values I learned in the BSA, such as honor, trustworthiness, and integrity, have served as my guiding principles in this business.

Today I consider myself to be one of Omaha's most knowledgeable investment property experts. I am not claiming to be #1 or #100, but I do know that I am good enough to succeed and help people from all walks of life to accomplish their own definition of the American dream. The expertise I have acquired as an investor has been invaluable for my clients, and I am able to back up my advice with real-life experiences.

I have bought and sold hundreds of properties over the years and still control an extensive rental property portfolio worth a few million dollars that generates a six-figure annual income. In other words, I walk the talk. Since 2003 I have flipped more than 50 properties and before that, at least 100 before the word "flipping" was even used. How times change.

I don't necessarily think of myself as a teacher, but I often conduct "Investing in Real Estate" seminars for people like you who are looking for a practical way to build financial security. I taught a course in real estate investing at a local real estate school for several years, and I am a provider of continuing education classes dealing with investments for agents approved by the Nebraska Real Estate Commission.

I am also proud to say that several of my former clients have become real estate agents as well. I feel fortunate to be able to do something I don't consider to be work, as I firmly believe that this is the best way to build wealth.

My hard work has paid off, and I am enjoying the "American Dream" of financial freedom. I am still making a very good living doing it, not because I must work but rather because I love what I do and I believe that helping people is my mission.

My mission: To help clients from all walks of life generate wealth so they are financially set up for their "golden years." To strive to always go above and beyond my clients' expectations by being a wealth advisor, coach, mentor, and the source of information for all their investment needs.

My vision: To be the real estate agent of choice for those who want to become financially independent.

My values: To always be 100% honest and never put my own needs before the needs of my clients. I know that when they make money, I will make money, so there's no need for me to worry about each commission check.

My legacy: To help real estate agents and clients by sharing my knowledge so that they can help others as well.

I have found that investing in real estate is the fastest path to financial independence for anyone from the executive to the blue-collar worker. Building wealth and making a living from the workplace are totally different pursuits. You can make a lot of money working for someone else and helping the owner get wealthy with no job security, or you can invest in real estate to build your own financial future. Which path sounds better to you? Being dependent or independent of the workplace?

I hope this book will motivate you if you have been on the fence about investing. Don't delay any longer. Find yourself a qualified agent who can guide you every step of the way and you will be glad you did. Remember that wealth is found on the other side of fear and real estate is the ticket to wealth building. Another way of putting it is "No risks, no rewards." If I can do it, so can you.

Why I wrote this book

When I was a novice investor in 1973, I knew absolutely nothing about real estate. Would I be in a different place today if Jerry Siciunas, my first real estate agent, hadn't taken me seriously?

I decided to write this book because I wanted to share my 45-plus years of knowledge and expertise with people like you, just as Jerry Siciunas did for me. If each of us had a mentor who took a little time to help us and if we then took the time to become a mentor to someone else, the world would be a better place.

When you look at the facts, you will see that investing in real estate is one of the better options for anyone desiring to become independently wealthy. Your goal, my goal, and in fact the goal of most people is not to rely on anyone else for their financial future.

- What would happen if you got sick and couldn't work for a few months? Would you have another source of income to tide you over until you were able to go back to work?
- Are you happy with the returns you are receiving from your current investments?
- Did you pay more than your fair share of taxes last year? I can pretty much guess how you responded, and I don't even know you. When I ask these questions, most people answer them as a red-flag need.

A real estate investment business not only will help you solve your financial concerns but also can be the ticket to becoming a millionaire. With a business plan, the right support team (real estate agent, attorney, accountant, banker/lender, contractors), and a strategy of investing wisely in properties that are worth owning, success will come more easily than you might imagine.

I have chosen to help clients and real estate agents to achieve financial success, and it is by far the most rewarding thing I have ever done. There is no better feeling than knowing you have helped a client to become a millionaire real estate investor.

By the time you finish reading this book, you will have a better understanding of all the investment options to consider, from single-family dwellings to multi-units, land development, commercial, industrial, manufacturing, hotels, motels, mobile home parks, shopping centers. You'll learn about the advantages and disadvantages of investing in each type of property so that you can make a more informed decision.

Depending on whom you talk to, you will get many different opinions as to which option is best. Always keep in mind that it is your money and your decision.

My own portfolio comprises houses and duplexes. You may ask why, and my reasoning is very simple. This type of real estate is easy to understand, and houses and duplexes will always be in demand. Other options require more responsibilities and are more difficult to understand and analyze. I am not saying they are good or bad, as it always is a personal preference.

Do you have the right real estate agent?

Before you begin to invest in real estate, your first step should be to find the right agent who has the experience and knowledge to guide you every step of the way. Your agent should know how to find deals on the MLS and analyze a property, and they should also be familiar with a wide range of topics including landlord issues, tenant-landlord laws, and financing options. Your agent should seek to understand your goals and then explain the advantages and disadvantages of all the investment choices available to you.

It's best to choose an agent who is also an investor so they will know the ins and out of this business and be able to give you the practical knowledge and expertise you deserve. They should subscribe to what they would like others to do. My guess is that you would not go to your family doctor if you are having heart issues. You certainly would make sure that the cardiologist is the very best one, and your agent should also be a specialist. Not all doctors are created equal, just as not every agent has the same level of expertise.

If you are not an investor yet, how long have you been thinking about starting a real estate investment business? What has kept you from jumping into this game? Is it a lack of confidence, insufficient knowledge, or do you see it as being too risky? Have you heard horror stories from people who failed because they didn't treat it as a business? Maybe they rented to the first person who had the deposit and rent in cash and drove a fancy car, and they didn't even have the tenant fill out a rental application. That is a pretty good clue it was going to be a disaster. I will cover in Chapter 3 why this business is likely to succeed while other small businesses are more likely to fail.

Follow my suggestions and you too will enjoy everything you have been dreaming about, including financial freedom.

Are you one of those people who wants to invest in real estate to gain control of your financial future because leaving it up to someone else is nerve-wracking? If you invest in real estate, you can take charge of your own financial future.

Is your workplace matching your 401K? Are they expecting more from you now than in the past? Are you working more hours than you would like? Are you underpaid or overpaid? Are you getting wealthy or just barely paying your bills? Are the company's owner, CEO, and top management receiving performance bonuses and becoming wealthier while you are lucky to get a pay raise?

I can identify with you because I have known people who were making a six-figure income and working long hours, then lost their job due to downsizing or because the company was sold.

I wish you much success if you decide to start today on your road to wealth building or adding to your portfolio. I hope this book will be the catalyst to help you become the next Millionaire Real Estate Investor. Remember, if I can do it so can you.

ACKNOWLEDGMENTS

This book is dedicated to the memory of my parents because they were wonderful role models who laid a strong foundation for the person that I am today.

Early on I watched them work hard to provide for my brother and me. They taught me that in order to get ahead you must make sacrifices, overcome obstacles, and have a deep passion and enthusiasm for whatever you are doing. They inspired me to become a high achiever, not to be afraid to try new things even if I might fail, to be courageous and give of myself to others.

My parents moved from Europe to Montevideo, Uruguay, in South America in the mid-1940s. From a young age, I was aware that they both worked extremely hard and had successful businesses. We had a very happy and normal life. They owned a nice home in a desirable neighborhood as well as a vacation home. Life was good for us, but they became concerned about the growing political unrest in Uruguay and decided to emigrate to the United States in 1963 when I was 12 years old. This was one of the most unselfish decisions they could have made, and to this day I continue to think "What if?" They came to this country because they wanted us to have the opportunity for a better life.

My parents instilled in me the drive to not let anything get in my way if I wanted something badly enough. I owe whatever financial success I have achieved to them. They taught me so many life lessons, yet it took me a long time to realize all that I learned.

They used to tell me, "You have to pay the price to succeed because nothing in life comes easily." I am the product of the American dream—proof that anything is possible in this country if you work hard and are willing to pay the price.

Although I did not understand it at the time, subconsciously all along I was telling myself that I would never rely on anyone else for my financial future and someday I would become financially independent.

In addition to my parents, another individual who inspired me to achieve was a family member who predicted that I would probably end up in jail and not amount to much. I wasn't a juvenile delinquent; I just got into trouble at school often. As a matter of fact, I had a chair reserved for me in the principal's and counselor's offices because I visited them regularly.

When I came to this country at 12 years old, I was scared to death and didn't speak English. I wanted attention, so I became the class clown. When I was in eighth grade the principal told my mother and this relative that the next time I got into trouble I would be kicked out of school. That got my attention.

I was aware that this family member had told my parents that I would end up in jail and not amount to much, and her prediction ended up having a big impact on my life because I didn't want her to be able to tell my parents "I told you so."

I used this negative chapter in my life to challenge myself and focus. Even in my adult life I never thanked this individual for helping me. I wanted so badly to prove she was wrong about me that it inspired me to succeed. I turned a negative into a positive.

So many people have inspired me and had so much influence on my real estate career that it would be impossible to thank them all individually. One person who comes to mind immediately is Jerry Siciunas, the real estate agent who helped me buy my first duplex in 1973. Jerry ignited my lifelong passion for real estate investing.

Finally, I want to thank my children, Kelly, Randi, and Ryan, for their support, encouragement, and belief in me. I am especially grateful that my daughter Kelly has joined me as a partner in my real estate practice.

A lot of people have helped me along the way, so when someone says they are self-made I don't think they are giving others the credit they deserve. First and foremost, nothing would have ever been possible without the people at Security National Bank who believed in me and loaned me the money I needed along the way. This has been a 35-year relationship. Of course, I also have other local lenders for the few properties that have loans. I am always asked if I know of some lender or accountant, attorney, contractor etc., and I only recommend to my clients businesses that I use personally.

Chapter 1

COULD REAL ESTATE BE YOUR PATH TO WEALTH?

Did you, or anyone close to you, lose money in the stock market during the economic downturn of 2008–2011?

Even if you didn't lose money in the stock market, are you satisfied with the interest on your savings or money market account? Are you actually able to spend the money you are earning on a monthly basis? Do you have any concerns in regard to the current economic situation?

I can assure you there's never a bad time to invest in real estate. Even during an economic downturn, real estate will continue to produce income because rental properties that are worth owning will always be in demand. This may not be true for other types of investments.

~

Throughout this book, I will show you why a real estate investment business is an effective and reliable investment option for most hard-working people. When I use the terms investor, real estate investor, and real estate investment business, they have the same meaning. For the purposes of this book a real estate investment is defined as ownership of a non-owner-occupied property.

~

No other investment option offers as many benefits as investing in real estate. These benefits include appreciation, principal reduction, rental income (cash flow), and tax reductions, but there are more important reasons why a real estate business is the ticket to wealth building, retirement income, and ultimately financial freedom.

When was the last time you considered where you are in your retirement planning? More people spend more time planning their next vacation than planning their retirement. Here are some questions to consider. If they apply to you, consider the "Big Why" you should give strong consideration to starting a real estate investing business:

- How comfortable are you with the current economic situation?
- Are you on track to accomplish your retirement objectives?
- How did you come out on your taxes last year? Did you pay more than you wanted?
- What are you planning to differently this year?
- How much longer do you plan on working? To retirement age?
- Will you have enough money to maintain your current lifestyle in retirement with your current income and/or investments?
- Are you prepared for life after work?
- What would happen if you got sick or became disabled and no longer could earn a living at the workplace?

- What is your current financial situation?
- Are you saving enough money regularly, or are you comfortable with your current savings?
- Do you have enough disposable income?
- Are you more in debt than you would like?
- Do you have a college savings plan for your children?
- Are you satisfied with the return from your current investments?

When you answered the questions above, did they raise concerns about your current financial situation? If so, a real estate investment business is your ticket to addressing any financial concerns you may have.

How many people are looking for ways to put their money to work? I have always wondered why more people from all walks of life are not investing in real estate. Do they steer clear of this type of investment due to a lack of knowledge or a sense of intimidation? Do they avoid real estate investment because they believe it's too risky?

Why do some people view real estate as a risky investment? Maybe they have a friend who lost money in real estate because they were unprepared and didn't have a knowledgeable agent assisting them. Maybe their friend bought a property they shouldn't have bought or paid too much for a property. Maybe they bought a property with very little cash flow in the hope that the value would appreciate over time. With the right preparation and guidance, none of these things would have happened. As I'll explain later in this book, the risk involved can be greatly minimized by buying undervalued properties that can be improved without spending huge amounts of money on the renovations.

I believe more people would invest in real estate if they knew the benefits it provides for wealth building and if more agents would provide this information to their current and past clients, friends, family members, neighbors, and others. I believe that everyone is a prospect and at a minimum, you are entitled to a conversation about how you could benefit from this business. Did the agent who sold you your house ever bring up the topic?

A savvy and knowledgeable real estate agent can help you understand that real estate doesn't have to be risky and instead can be one of the better investment options available. According to Martin Thomas, investor and CEO of Opportunity–Investor.com, eight out of ten millionaires surveyed became wealthy through real estate. That means an overwhelming proportion of the people we'd like to emulate earned their wealth by trading in real estate.

A large percentage of the world's richest individuals credit much of their wealth to investing in real estate in one form or another. My guess is that early in their investment history all of them utilized the services of a real estate agent.

Ten Richest Real Estate Investors in the United States

The combined net worth of the top ten real estate investors in the United States is a whopping $123 billion, according to Wealth-X, a global provider of information on the high-net-worth community. (Net worth and ranking data provided by Wealth-X.)

1. Donald Bren – Net Worth: $15.2B – Base of Operations: Southern California

2. Stephen Ross – Net Worth: $6.6B – Base of Operations: New York

3. Richard LeFrak – Net Worth: $6.1B – Base of Operations: New York

4. Ted Lerner – Net Worth: $5.4B – Base of Operations: Chevy Chase, MD

5. John A. Sobrato – Net Worth: $4.9B – Base of Operations: Atherton, CA

6. Sam Zell – Net Worth: $4.8B – Base of Operations: Chicago

7. Leonard Stern – Net Worth: $4.6B – Base of Operations: New York

8. Donald Trump – Net Worth: $4B – Base of Operations: New York

9. Jerry Speyer – Net Worth: $4.4B – Base of Operations: New York

10. Edward Roski Jr. – Net Worth: $3.9B Base of Operations: Los Angeles

Although you may never become a billionaire like the investors on the list, you can become a millionaire real estate investor if you are creditworthy.

Are you the perfect prospect to invest in real estate?

Are you creditworthy and looking for financial security? Are you a high-net-worth individual looking for tax benefits? Are you an hourly wage earner looking for additional income?

Without even knowing you, I have a feeling that you could also benefit by investing in real estate. Each person has specific needs and objectives, whether they are looking for cash flow or tax benefits.

How many people do you know who consistently complain about the amount of taxes they are paying every year yet do nothing about it? How many people have taken part-time jobs (in addition to their full-time occupation) to make ends meet?

Has your accountant ever suggested that you explore the option of investing in real estate? What about your financial advisor? If they have your best interests in mind, they will tell you that real estate is where it's at.

Real estate investors reduce the impact of economic downturns

When you purchased your first home, most likely you saw it as a place to raise a family and create some memories. Looking down the road, you realized that at some point your house would be paid off and you would be able to sell it and perhaps buy another home.

Unfortunately, for some homeowners the downturn in the real estate market over the past ten to twelve years took a toll on their home equity. The ones who were hit hardest were people who had paid too much for their property, borrowed 100% or 125% of the purchase price, or taken out subprime loans. Fortunately, today we are seeing an uptick in the market. Real estate has always been recognized as a positive alternative for building wealth, as it has done for me for more than 45 years. Today, real estate is a more popular investment choice than any other.

In communities throughout our country, investors played a major role in stabilizing the residential market by purchasing foreclosed properties during the downturn. Although the impact of the recession was unfortunate for those who lost their homes to foreclosure, the savvy investors who purchased these properties made huge profits and will continue to do so for years to come.

Building wealth by investing in real estate is certainly not easy. If it took no effort at all, everyone would be doing it. It takes hard work and sacrifice, but you don't have to be a genius to be successful. Genuine desire goes a long way.

Buying and holding income-producing properties is the ticket to wealth building. People who choose this path can create a sizable portfolio that will generate residual income for many years to come.

How confident are you with the current economic outlook? My guess is that you are no different from many others who are uncertain about what the future will bring.

While our economic future may be uncertain, more than 45 years of being a real estate investor have taught me that the opportunities are endless. When you invest in real estate and have the right agent, you should be able to purchase undervalued properties that can be fixed up and either rented or "flipped."

In my experience, income-producing properties offer higher returns with lower risks than any other investment option. Keep in mind that with real estate YOU are in control of your assets, not your stockbroker or financial planner or anyone else.

I am sure you personally know individuals who have made a lot of money by operating their own business, but are they creating wealth or just paying their bills?

Do you know anybody who thought they had the right business model and went for the "American Dream" and lost everything in a business that failed?

While chasing money for the sake of chasing money may not give you long-term satisfaction, how would it feel that if you didn't have to worry about money and could even leave a legacy for your children or give money to your favorite charity?

How many people do you know who are happy even though they have money concerns and can't pay their bills?

Assume that wherever you are investing your money, whether in the stock market or other options, you are doing it with the idea that someday your investments will replace the income from your work and allow you to live comfortably in retirement.

How satisfied are you from the returns you are receiving from investments? If not, what are you doing about it? How much of the dividends you are earning are you able to spend on a monthly basis: $100, $200, $10,000, $20,000, $30,000 or more? Real estate can generate this kind of cash flow on a monthly basis. You can spend it and still have the property or portfolio working hard for you 24/7. You can even do this on a part-time basis while keeping your current job.

How many ordinary, hard-working individuals do you know who view the prospect of becoming wealthy and financially independent as more of a dream than reality? This business model is the real deal.

If you have been sitting on the sidelines, I cncourage you to find yourself the right agent who can guide you every step of the way. I guarantee that you will be glad you did. Who would not be interested in exploring how they can build wealth so that someday they can be worry-free?

Every type of investment including real estate goes through cycles and may encounter setbacks along the way, just as we have seen in the past few years with declining property values. But for investors who purchased undervalued properties, or even those who paid market price, all the benefits of real estate ownership are still hard at work (cash flow, tax savings, appreciation, principal reduction). And how about the fact that their mortgage is being reduced every month because of rental income? These are some of the reasons why my personal wealth will continue to be invested in real estate.

Wealth building through real estate is not a quick-fix solution. Instead, one must look several years down the road to a time when these properties will be paid in full. Think about the residual income that will continue for the rest of your life.

Although the possibilities are endless, someone who has little knowledge and lacks the assistance of an experienced real estate agent could make a huge mistake. Very quickly their dream of achieving financial independence could become a nightmare.

Will you be able to afford a comfortable lifestyle in retirement?

It used to be that you could work for a company for 30 years and expect to retire with a nice pension. Unfortunately, the workplace no longer offers that kind of job security. Retirement pensions have dwindled, and the value of many 401(K)s has greatly diminished. Today's employees will be lucky to get a gold watch when they retire.

I can recall my father working extremely hard in the 1960s and '70s at a job that paid the minimum wage. His employer did not offer a retirement plan, and I can't remember whether he had insurance coverage.

But fortunately, my parents had enough wisdom to invest in three rental properties in the 1970s that provided $1,500 monthly residual income for many years until they sold them and had a little more security for their golden years.

The bottom line is that retirement prospects are not looking very good for many people, and economic uncertainty is greatly affecting the amount of money that is being saved. People are concerned that they might lose their job, some are underemployed, and others are unemployed and using the funds they set aside for retirement just to make ends meet.

How many people do you know who lost money in the stock market, 401(K) accounts, pension plans, and so on? Although the economy has rebounded recently, most of these investments are still a long way from reaching the same value they had a few years ago.

The picture is the opposite for investors who purchased undervalued properties during the past few years. They gained instant equity by buying properties considered to be a good deal and began earning ongoing income from long-term rentals. These same properties made great flippers.

If the thought-provoking question struck a chord ,when is it going to be the right time to get a handle on your retirement planning? Ouch—all of a sudden you are 65 years of age and then it's too late.

Many employees can no longer afford to contribute to their 401(K), so they are missing out on employer matching. If they had invested in a rental property, the benefits would have been tremendous: rental income, tax savings and perhaps even a fully paid property producing monthly residual income in the form of rent.

What about the rising cost of medical care and health insurance, which has caused many to dip into their retirement funds to pay medical bills? How many of your close friends or family members would fall into this category?

The saddest news of all is that retirement statistics are very scary, as the net worth of most Americans has diminished dramatically. As you consider the retirement statistics on the next few pages, think about how applicable they are to your own situation. Note: While the research and statistics may differ from source to source, the information should give an indication of the financial situation for many Americans.

According to a report published in September 2018 by the National Institute on Retirement Income (Retirement Crisis Persists Despite Economic Recovery), the retirement savings of working-age Americans remain deeply inadequate. An analysis of U.S. Census Bureau data reveals that the median retirement account balance among all working individuals is $0. The data also indicate that 57% of working-age individuals do not own any retirement account assets in an employer-sponsored 401(k)-type plan, individual account, or pension.

The analysis finds that overall, four out of five working Americans have less than one year's income saved in retirement accounts. Also, 77% of Americans fall short of conservative retirement savings targets for their age based on working until age 67, even if the total amount saved includes an individual's entire net worth—a generous measure of retirement savings. Moreover, a large majority of working-age Americans cannot meet even a substantially reduced savings target.

Growing income inequality widens the gap in retirement account ownership. Workers in the top income quartile are five times more likely to have retirement accounts than workers in the lowest income quartile. And individuals with retirement accounts have, on average, more than three times the annual income of individuals who do not have retirement accounts.

These statistics suggest that the American dream of a modest retirement after a lifetime of work has become out of reach for the average worker. Even among workers who were able to put some of their money in retirement accounts, the typical worker had an account balance of only $40,000. This falls far short of the savings levels Americans will need if they hope to sustain their standard of living in retirement.

Every day, the choices we make either bring us closer to or farther away from financial freedom.

The retirement savings shortfall can be attributed to a multitude of factors and a breakdown of the nation's retirement infrastructure. There is a massive retirement plan coverage gap among American workers. Fewer workers have stable and secure pensions, 401(k)-style defined contribution (DC) individual accounts provide fewer savings and protection, and increases in the Social Security retirement age translate into lower retirement income.

The catastrophic financial crisis of 2008 exposed the vulnerability of the DC-centered retirement system. Many Americans saw the value of their retirement plans plummet when the financial markets crashed and destroyed trillions of dollars of household wealth. Asset values in Americans' retirement accounts fell from $9.3 trillion at the end of 2007 to $7.2 trillion at the end of 2008.

The economic downturn also triggered a decline in total contributions to DC retirement accounts as many employers stopped matching employee contributions for a time, pushing total contributions below 2008 levels. Since then, the combined value of 401(k)-type accounts and IRAs reached $16.9 trillion by the end of 2017. Unfortunately, this increase in total retirement account assets has not improved retirement security for most American workers and their families who have nothing saved.

In this uncertain environment, Americans face an ongoing quandary: how much income will they need if they retire, and can they ever save enough money to meet that need? To maintain their standard of living in retirement, the typical working American needs to replace roughly 85% of pre-retirement income. Social Security, under the current benefit formula, provides a replacement rate of roughly 35% for a typical worker. This leaves a retirement income gap equal to 50% of pre-retirement earnings that must be filled through other means.

As you consider these statistics, which ones are relevant to you? If you are not on track for a comfortable retirement, what are you going to do about it? If you continue to do what you have always done, you can't expect different results. Wealth is found on the other side of fear. So what do you have to lose by trying?

Real estate investment is a realistic way to build wealth

Real estate is one of the few investment options available to people from all walks of life.

How realistic is the stock market as a path to wealth for someone who has only $10,000 or $20,000 to invest? But anyone who is creditworthy can get a loan and use other people's money (OPM) to make a down payment of 20% to 25% and control a $100,000 property. How powerful would this asset be to an hourly worker in 10, 15, or 20 years when the property is paid off? How many people do you know who have $100,000 in their savings account? It is a lot easier than you might think to amass a sizable real estate portfolio. Good credit is paramount, however.

Compared with the stock market, it is quite easy to invest in real estate if you have good credit, a solid financial statement, and collateral (such as equity on your personal residence or from other rental properties). Possibly you can get a line of credit or bridge loan. Offers can be written as cash if the collateral is not tied to the subject property. The assumption is that the undervalued property needs some type of work to improve its value. Once the property has been improved, it can be refinanced and the owner might even be able to pull out 100% of the money that was invested—the purchase price plus fix-up costs. Likely when the improvements have been made, the property will be worth far more than its purchase price. Let's say the purchase price of a property is $60,000 and you spend $20,000 improving it. Your total investment is $80,000. If the property appraises for $115,000, you can refinance the original investment amount ($80,000) and have $35,000 in equity to use for a down payment or college fund or some other purpose. The above example is used as an illustration and I am aware that real estate values in your community may be much higher. Omaha, Nebraska, is a great place to invest because of its affordable real estate, and you might want to consider purchasing property here if real estate prices in your community are prohibitive.

~

Making a lot of money is no guarantee of financial security. The secret is not how much money one makes but how much money one keeps and invests wisely.

~

Buying and holding income-producing properties is the most realistic way for most people to build wealth with minimum risk. In a later chapter we will discuss how to minimize risk by analyzing a property before buying it.

Changes in the value of real estate are much more predictable than those of other investments such as stocks. Furthermore, real estate offers control for the investor. With other forms of investments, you must rely on someone else to handle your money.

I realize that money can be made in the stock market or by gambling in a casino or by buying a winning lottery ticket, but how realistic are those paths to wealth for most of us?

Yes, there will be challenges along the way, such as unexpected expenses, poor tenant selection resulting in damage to the property, vacant properties, and so on, but the advantages are well worth it. Most of us want to be in control of our future, and real estate offers just that.

Keep the following principle in mind as you are reading this book: When you invest in real estate, you make your money when you buy (by purchasing properties that are undervalued or considered to be a deal). A rental property is not like day trading. Rather, it is a long-term investment. In 15 to 20 years the tenant ultimately pays off your mortgage and then you continue to receive residual income in the form of rent for years to come. What a wonderful concept!

Maybe you are an investor already, so you understand the impact of real estate investment on wealth building. I am one of those who has been greatly blessed by this industry. I have helped a lot of clients to attain financial freedom, and I did this by providing the expertise and knowledge they did not yet have.

~

Don't wait to buy real estate—Buy real estate and wait. —T. HARV EKER

Over 90% of all millionaires became so through owning real estate. —ANDREW CARNEGIE

Every person who invests in well-selected real estate in a growing section of a prosperous community adopts the surest and safest method of becoming independent, for real estate is the basis for wealth. —THEODORE ROOSEVELT (1858–1919)

~

A real estate investment business is an excellent way for most hardworking people to become millionaires. Working for someone else is a way to make a living without any job security, and investing in real estate can be a terrific source of additional income and ultimately a path to financial independence.

Financial independence does not have to be a dream for you. If you treat real estate investment as a business, you can become a millionaire and retire early. I can assure you that the possibility is very real and within your reach. This is not a quick-fix gimmick. If you have good credit and you are willing to make some sacrifices now, you will be rewarded. Real estate is the avenue to wealth, no matter what city you live in, your education, or background.

I encourage you to take the next step and find the right real estate agent. Call a few of the real estate agencies in your community and ask the broker who they recommend and why. Make sure you ask if the agent they recommend owns any rental properties and/or has flipped some properties.

Think about it: If over the next ten years you purchase two properties yearly, you will ultimately control 20 properties, and when they are fully paid for they will be worth a few million dollars, earning six-figure residual income for years to come. How powerful would that be for you? Ultimately, the tenant is the one who made you wealthy.

What form of investment allows you to make money while enjoying generous deductions such as tax benefits? Stocks? No. Real estate? Yes. In a later chapter, we will cover the tax benefits in detail, including depreciation, maintenance, and so on. One of the most powerful methods the IRS provides is the 1031 tax exchange, which allows you to defer capital gains.

Real estate will continue to be one of the most consistently lucrative and favorable models for wealth building. Shelter will always be a necessity, and investing in residential property has met the test of time.

While there are many things to consider before making the decision to invest in real estate, you need to understand the different strategies that are available to you. With some you will build wealth, and with others you can make a living. You should decide which strategy is best for you, keeping in mind that it is possible to do both. Do you want to buy and flip, buy and hold, or wholesale for a quick profit? What are your long-term and short-term objectives?

How to build a worthwhile real estate portfolio

Investors who make a lot of money in real estate and have a sizable net worth follow a plan. They don't leave things to chance. Below is a step-by-step guide for building a worthwhile real estate portfolio.

Step 1: Develop a business plan. Real estate investment is a business whether you have one property or 100. A sample business plan is provided in Chapter 13.

Step 2: Make good, practical decisions right from the start. Become a student of this "game" and learn as much as possible before you make your first deal. Develop a working relationship with a real estate agent who has expertise and is an investor.

Step 3: Look for properties in family-friendly neighborhoods. The right property attracts the right tenants or buyers. Try to find the worst-looking property on the best block, since you can make many changes to a property but you can never change its location.

Step 4: Develop a relationship with a local bank.

Step 5: Decide how much financial risk you are willing to take. Real estate requires money, and most of the time the funds will be borrowed from a bank. Get comfortable with the financial numbers and concentrate on increasing your property values.

Step 6: If you do not yet own any investment properties, a good way to begin is to purchase a single-family home or duplex.

Step 7: Fix up your property. This may include exterior paint, updating the kitchen and baths, landscaping, and so on. Try to hire a contractor who can do most of the work. Nicely updated properties will merit much higher rents and better tenants. Find out if remodeling will require a permit.

Step 8: Keep your personal expenses low. Reinvest any profits to grow your holdings.

Step 9: Continue purchasing properties as you become more and more comfortable with the process and have the financial resources to do so.

Step 10: Diversify your holdings. For example, you might want to acquire a mix of properties such as houses, duplexes, fourplexes, and so on.

Step 11: Rent only to tenants who meet your criteria (favorable credit report, criminal check, landlord verification, employment history).

Overall tips and warnings for new investors

When you are getting started as an investor, it's a good idea to interview several local banks to determine which one will give you the best terms. Your best option will often be a locally owned bank rather than a nationwide bank. Getting a loan with a favorable interest rate is only one aspect to consider. Can you establish a line of credit? If so, this will allow you to pay cash for properties upfront. It is important that you buy undervalued properties so you can raise the value by remodeling and then term them out (obtain a permanent loan for the property).

The real estate industry is filled with "get-rich-quick" programs that sell empty promises at exorbitant prices. Your best strategy as a new investor is to work with a reputable real estate agent who has firsthand experience and familiarity with the local real estate market. They can guide you step-by-step and offer practical advice instead of theoretical ideas.

Whatever you do, take the first step. If you don't get off the starting block, you will never be on the road to generating wealth. Buy today so you can profit tomorrow.

Key points to remember:

- ✓ Investing in real estate is less risky than putting your money into the stock market, and it gives you greater control of your assets.
- ✓ Risk can be minimized through careful planning and good advice from a residential real estate investment specialist.
- ✓ Real estate continues to produce income even during economic downturns.
- ✓ The long-term prospects for receiving income from rental properties are excellent because housing will always be in demand.

Chapter 2

WHAT ARE THE BENEFITS OF INVESTING IN REAL ESTATE?

Most likely, you have been putting some of your income in a savings or retirement account on a regular basis. Maybe you also own bonds, stocks, or gold. And if you're not already investing in real estate, I hope this book will convince you to get started.

When you think about it, why do you save or invest in the first place? I assume that you are still working and your goal is to have enough retirement income to maintain your current lifestyle.

How often do you think about whether you will have enough money to enjoy your retirement? Do you feel confident that you'll be able to travel or do the things on your bucket list?

You are working hard right now so that someday your money will work hard for you. You are counting on your investment portfolio to provide the income to support your needs and lifestyle.

How many people do you know for whom the opposite is true? They make a decent income and perhaps earn more than $100,000 per year but have no real savings or retirement plan and are living from paycheck to paycheck. Retirement is just a dream for them. This scenario probably applies to many of your neighbors, family members, and friends.

Although the economic crisis raised awareness of the importance of retirement planning, millions of Americans still have a dismal outlook regarding their ability to retire.

Luckily, there is a path out of financial insecurity. Investing in real estate puts you in control of your retirement income, and for some investors it can change their retirement outlook from dismal to optimistic. How does real estate fit into your financial future?

Different generations have different reasons for buying and selling real estate

In March 2018, LendEDU conducted a survey that asked people to answer the following question.

Question: If you were given $10,000 tax-free and had the ability to invest all of it in one of the following options, which would you choose?

Here are the results of the sample as a whole:

HOW TO INVEST $10K?	% OF RESPONDENTS
Pay down debt	27.3
Real estate	13.5
Savings account or CDs	12.2
401(k) or Roth IRA	9.9
Stock market	7.2
Child's education	6.9
Small business	6.2
Virtual currency	5.1
Education	3.2
Other/Unsure	8.5

Note: We've made slight adjustments to the original answers, moving one low-performing category (P2P loans) into the "Other" category.

Paying down debt (27.3%) was by far the most popular response. Real estate (13.5%) came in second. It's interesting to see that some people would opt to put the $10K toward their own small business, education, or even digital currencies like Bitcoin, Ethereum, or Litecoin.

How close are you to retirement? Your age is likely to affect your opinions of different investments. The following table shows the same survey data grouped by generations:

How to Invest $10K?	Millennials (< 35)	Gen X (35–54)	Boomers 55+
Pay down debt	22.4%	25.3%	33.1%
Real estate	15.1%	14.6%	11.2%
Education	9.9%	1.1%	0.3%
Virtual currency	9.2%	4.0%	3.1%
401(k) or Roth IRA	8.5%	9.4%	11.5%
Other/Unsure	8.1%	8.6%	8.7%
Savings account or CDs	7.7%	10.8%	17.1%
Stock market	6.6%	8.1%	6.7%
Child's education	6.3%	11.3%	2.8%
Small business	6.3%	6.7%	5.6%

Interestingly, certain answers were basically the same for all generations.

All groups were equally interested in investing in their own small business. The highest response here came from Gen X at 6.7%, but Millennials and Gen X weren't far behind at 6.3% and 5.6%, respectively.

Investing in the stock market was consistent as well, with Millennials at 6.6%, Generation X at 8.1%, and Boomers at 6.7%.

Some generational differences are predictable. For instance, barely any Baby Boomers (0.3%) wanted to put $10,000 toward their own education. This makes sense since many are at or near retirement age. On the other hand, 9.9% of Millennials opted for investing in their own education.

But here's a situation that might seem a bit more peculiar. One would guess that with student debt being at $1.5 trillion in the United States, many Millennials would opt to pay down debt with their $10,000 check. Interestingly, fewer Millennials (22.4%) chose to pay down debt than either Gen X (25.3%) or Boomers (33.1%).

Millennials were more likely than the other two groups to choose either real estate (15.1%) or cryptocurrency (9.2%) as an investment. By contrast, 11.2% of Boomers chose real estate and only 3.1% chose cryptocurrency.

Millennials (18- to 34-year-olds) understand that real estate is a good investment

Americans have stashed the majority of their investment dollars in the stock market over the years. But there may be a new trend on the horizon. In 2007, nearly two-thirds of Americans were investing in the stock market, but ten years later just over half did.

Realty Shares recently teamed up with Harris Interactive to compile a Real Estate Investing Report surveying Americans on their investment preferences. According to the survey results, 55% of Millennials are interested in investing in real estate, the highest percentage of all demographics questioned. Research from Fannie Mae supports these findings, reporting that 85% of Millennials think real estate is a good investment. With such a strong preference for real estate, it is important to understand why Millennials are interested and how they are likely to invest in the future.

Why is this information so important? In 2016 Millennials became the largest generation of Americans. As the largest age group, Millennials will have the greatest ability to shift the real estate market as their net worth builds.

In the Realty Shares survey, 20% of Millennials indicated that they believe real estate has performed better than the stock market since 2000. In fact, Millennials were the age group with the largest percentage holding that belief. The next highest group to believe real estate had outperformed the stock market since 2000 is Generation X (ages 35–44), 16% of whom chose real estate as the top performer.

Why are Millennials likely to value real estate over the stock market? Many Millennials graduated from college and entered the job market during the Great Recession. This major economic downturn made it difficult for them to find jobs. Simultaneously, they watched the stock market undergo the worst crash since the Great Depression. Although the burst of the housing bubble contributed to the stocks' crashing, the stock market crash may have lingered in people's minds longer than the problems with the housing market did.

Gen Xers (35- to 54-year-olds) are transitioning from renters to homeowners

Gen Xers are the members of the generation between the Baby Boomers and Millennials. This group is smaller and less influential than Baby Boomers and Millennials, but in recent years it has had a significant effect on real estate. It's important to remember that Gen Xers suffered terribly during the 2009 housing crash, and many lost their homes. Therefore until a few years ago, the majority of Gen Xers have stuck to renting homes. But if there's one thing they're proving, it's that they no longer want to solely rent property. With a stronger U.S. economy, an ever-growing job market, and increasing home values, more Gen Xers are taking the leap into property ownership.

Why is it important to track Gen Xers and understand their effect on real estate? Simply put, Gen Xers have higher incomes than either Baby Boomers or Millennials. Because they're in their prime money-making years, they can afford to buy property. Many are trading their smaller homes for larger, more luxurious ones.

The National Association of Realtors' Home Buyer and Generational Trends study for 2017 showed that the proportion of Generation X home-buyers grew from 26% to 28%. As this percentage increases over time, Gen X's effect on real estate will become more substantial.

It's important to remember that while they make the most money, Gen Xers are not the largest segment of home buyers in the United States. Millennials take the title for that one.

Baby Boomers (age 55 and up) love to invest in real estate

The primary reason Boomers invest in property is to protect their assets from the negative impact of inflation. History shows that property prices tend to increase at a faster rate than inflation over the long term. With this in mind, many Boomers are pulling their money out of low-interest savings accounts and investing it in real estate.

DEPPRO (Depreciation Professionals) has found that most Boomer investors are planning to retire within the next decade (if they haven't already retired) and therefore need to ensure that their investment returns exceed the inflation rate over this period. With life expectancies now increasing, many Boomers are concerned that their savings alone may not provide enough funds during their retirement years, which could last more than two decades.

Baby Boomer property investors have been very active in the property market because they are highly informed about property investment opportunities. Many have been involved in the property market for many years by owning their own home and therefore understand the long-term capital growth rates that property ownership can deliver. An increasing number of Boomers now view real estate investment as a less risky option than the stock market to build wealth for their retirement.

Many Boomers are leveraging the large amounts of equity they have in their owner-occupied homes to organize home loans in excess of $1 million and purchase several investment properties. Over the past year, DEPPRO has undertaken property depreciation reports for Boomers who own as many as seven or eight investment properties. DEPPRO has found that many Boomers are highly informed about property investment opportunities and know that they can fund their investment strategy through tax incentives such as negative gearing and property depreciation. For example, a number of DEPPRO's Baby Boomer clients receive tax refunds in excess of $50,000 for the first five financial years after completing a depreciation report on their investment property.

How can investing in real estate improve your financial outlook?

As mentioned in Chapter 1, in this book "investment real estate" is defined as property that generates income or is otherwise intended for investment purposes rather than as a primary residence. It is common for investors to own multiple pieces of real estate, one of which serves as a primary residence while the others are used to generate rental income and profits through price appreciation. The tax implications of investing in real estate are often different from those for homeowners.

Real estate is a commodity in which people invest their hard-earned money with the expectation that they will receive profits. These profits can be achieved in many ways, including rental income, principal reduction, appreciation, and "flipping" or reselling for a profit.

Historically, real estate has shown consistent growth in value. This growth occurs even during periods when other investment choices are less desirable.

In the short term, real estate can be a wonderful investment because of the money that can be made by flipping. For example, you might pay $100,000 to purchase a home that needs work. Your total cost for rehabbing, holding cost, commissions, and so on is $35,000. Four months later, you sell the home for $180,000, earning a profit of $55,000 (less the selling costs and taxes to Uncle Sam). How many people do you know who can make that kind of money in such a short time? Some people work for an entire year without earning $55,000. Keep in mind that the profits will be treated as ordinary income for tax purposes, so check with your accountant to determine the amount you will owe in taxes.

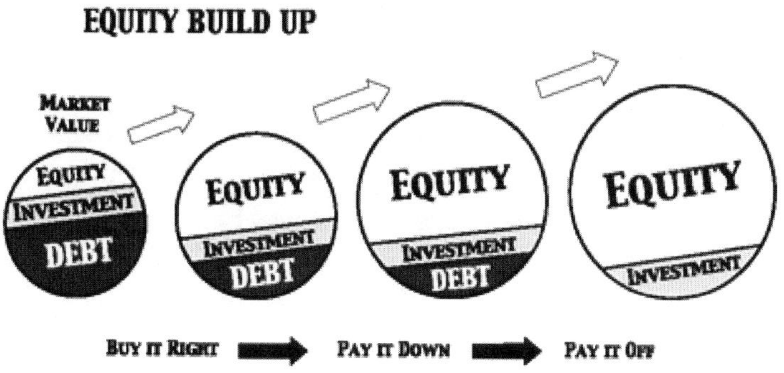

EQUITY BUILD UP

Buy it Right → Pay it Down → Pay it Off

Rental property, on the other hand, works well as a long-term purchase. When you buy a rental property, your tenant ultimately is the one who reduces your mortgage balance. Building equity is the name of the game, and increased net worth is the outcome.

Real estate investors need to figure out whether they are looking for short-term profits (to make a living) or long-term equity (to build wealth). Their answer will determine the type of property they buy.

Additionally, income-producing properties can serve different purposes for different investors. For example, a prudent way to supplement retirement income might be to start acquiring rental properties long before age 65 so that when the mortgages are paid off the investor can live off the residual income during retirement.

For a different investor, a more aggressive plan might be a better choice. This type of person might want to acquire a sizable portfolio of properties that generate enough cash flow that he or she will not have to rely on income from the workplace—the American dream of entrepreneurship in action.

Why should you start your own real estate investment business?

Here are just a few reasons why real estate is one of the best investments around: leverage, positive cash flow, wealth building, hedge against inflation, portfolio diversification, tax deductions, 1031 exchange, tax-free cash refinance, and being your own boss. Each of these benefits is described briefly below and also covered in detail later in this book.

➢ ***Leverage***

Leverage is the use of borrowed funds to finance and accumulate real estate. Leveraging lets the investor use other people's money (OPM) to acquire properties. This is one of the most powerful tools investors can utilize because it allows them to purchase and finance increasing numbers of properties. Through leverage, they can substantially increase their return on investment (ROI). Gaining access to OPM is easy if the investor has a solid financial statement and is creditworthy. ....

Few other investment options allow a person to make money on borrowed money. Based on a typical down payment of 20% to 25%, the potential profit on real estate is considerably greater than the profit for a non-leveraged investment such as stocks or mutual funds. You can't use leverage to buy stocks unless you have a significant cash reserve and a very strong financial statement. (You may have heard the term margin, which refers to borrowing money from your broker to buy stock and using the stock as collateral.)

What happens when someone loses money on margin? A loss of 50 percent or more from stocks bought on margin equates to a loss of 100 percent or more, plus interest and commissions. In that scenario, you lose all of your own money, plus interest and commissions. In addition, the equity in your account has to maintain a certain value called the maintenance margin.

➢ ***Positive cash flow***

Real estate should be a cash-generating investment over the long term. When you rent a property to a qualified tenant (having done due diligence in tenant selection to minimize risk), the rent payments should more than cover the mortgage payments, taxes, insurance, and maintenance. After these expenses are paid, the investment provides cash flow or residual income before taxes to Uncle Sam. When the property is paid in full, it is an excellent source of retirement income. How many people do you know who make $200 and up in dividends from investments other than real estate and can actually spend the money without being taxed?

➢ ***Wealth building***

Historically real estate has increased in value and should continue to do so over time. In later chapters, we will cover what classifies a property as a good investment that will build wealth over time, how and where to find such properties, and how to fund investment property.

A real estate investment can build wealth in the following ways:

- Appreciation: Real estate tends to go up and down in value, but the long-term trend is upward. Why? The answer involves supply and demand. As Mark Twain said, "Buy land—they're not making it anymore." If the population of the United States continues to rise, good rental properties will always be in demand. And rents will tend to go up as well, especially if the property is well maintained and located in a desirable area.

- Cash flow: When a property is rented for income, there should be more income coming in than expenses going out.

- Tax benefits: Deductions should offset the investor's tax liability for income from other sources (salary and other investments). (Note: Anyone contemplating the purchase of real estate should seek the services of a competent legal professional and tax advisor.)

- Principle reduction: As you make payments on a mortgage, each month the amount owed decreases slightly until the last payment is made and the loan is paid in full.

➢ ***A hedge against inflation***

Real estate is one of the few assets that react proportionately to inflation. As inflation occurs, housing values increase and rents go up. Although some people see real estate as a risky investment, I believe real estate is one of the only safe investments left, given our ongoing financial crisis. Unlike the stock market, you can't lose all the money you have invested in a rental property.

➢ ***Portfolio diversification***

As part of your investment portfolio, real estate allows you to avoid putting all of your eggs in one basket. Most investment professionals agree that diversification will help you reach your long-range financial goals while minimizing risk. The key to successful diversification is finding a happy medium between risk and return.

Investments in each of the following asset categories do different things for you:

- Stocks help your portfolio grow.

- Bonds bring you income.

- Cash gives your portfolio security and stability.

- Real estate provides both a hedge against inflation and low "correlation" to stocks—in other words, the value of your real estate may rise during times when stock values fall.

➢ ***Tax deductions***

When you or your accountant prepared your income tax returns last year, how happy were you with the amount of taxes you paid? More than likely, you felt that you paid too much tax because you didn't have enough deductions. Most taxpayers probably feel the same way.

Don't get me wrong—I think paying taxes is a good thing because it means I am making money. But I believe in paying no more than my fair share of taxes. After all, the amount of money we make is less important than how much we get to keep.

One of the best things about being a real estate investor is the many federal income tax advantages that become available to you. The Internal Revenue Service treats rental properties as a business venture, and therefore expenses involved in being a landlord are tax deductible. For details, see the "Tax Deductions for Real Estate Investors" summary in the Resources section at the end of this book.

➢ ***1031 tax-deferred exchange***

If a real estate investment is no longer meeting your needs or you want to increase leverage and free up equity, you should consider a 1031 tax-deferred exchange. Normally, when property is sold, any gain on the sale will be taxed. However, the 1031 exchange allows you to defer capital gains tax on the sale of real estate when you use the proceeds to purchase any type of real estate. This tax deferral can provide you with capital to invest in a subsequent purchase.

▹*Refinancing*

As rents and property values continue to go up, refinancing can be used to purchase additional properties if the appraisal will substantiate the value. For example, let's say a property appraises for $100,000 and has a mortgage balance of $40,000. With a loan-to-value (LTV) ratio of 80%, the amount that you can pull out by refinancing your mortgage is $40,000 less refinance expenses

Is it better to pay off the loan or refinance? The answer depends on your age, acquisition objectives, and other factors.

▹ ***Being your own boss***

One of the most powerful advantages of owning real estate is the fact that you become your own boss. As a real estate investor, you get to choose which properties you will invest in, which tenants you will rent to, how much rent you will charge, and how you will manage and maintain the property. This is very different from working at a job where you must do what your supervisor wants you to do. And when you work hard at a job you are making the owner of the company wealthy, not increasing your own net worth.

Lots of people buy stocks in companies or shares in mutual funds without understanding why the value of their investment goes up or down. Who knows what the CEO or other people in the company are doing with your money? But as a real estate investor, you are in control, and the entire responsibility for the success or failure of your investment rests with you.

Real estate is a tangible asset. You can see it, drive by it, and improve it. You get to decide what to do or not do with it, and you will reap the benefits of your decisions.

About 90% of those who are considered millionaires made their money through real estate. On February 27, 2012, Warren Buffett (the "Oracle of Omaha") described single-family homes as a very attractive investment. He said he would buy up "a couple hundred thousand" single-family homes if it were practical to do so. If houses are purchased at low rates and held for a long time, Buffett explained, they are a better investment than stocks.

The BIG WHY for real estate investing

As I will emphasize throughout this book, the BIG WHY for real estate investing should be to build wealth, retirement income, and financial freedom. If you're not on track to accomplish your retirement objectives, what are you planning to do differently? Keep in mind that at the end of the day, the choices you make will either bring you closer to your goals or farther away from achieving financial freedom.

I am very confident that if you subscribe to the BIG WHY and choose your properties carefully and intelligently, investing in real estate can yield substantial benefits that cannot be achieved through any other type of investment. Ultimately, you will attain financial freedom.

Key points to remember:

- ✓ The main reason people save or invest part of their earnings is to maintain their current lifestyle during retirement.
- ✓ Different generations have different reasons for buying and selling real estate.
- ✓ As an investment, real estate offers more profit, greater control, and lower risk than stocks.
- ✓ Improving undervalued properties and selling them can bring substantial short-term profits, while holding income-producing property for decades builds wealth over the long term.
- ✓ Owners of rental property can control their retirement income or become less dependent on making a living from the workplace.
- ✓ Real estate investments can provide benefits that include leverage, positive cash flow, wealth building, hedge against inflation, appreciation, portfolio diversification, tax deductions, 1031 exchange or tax-free cash refinance, and being your own boss.
- ✓ The "big why" to invest in real estate should be to build wealth, retirement income, and financial freedom.

Chapter 3

REAL ESTATE VERSUS A TRADITIONAL SMALL BUSINESS

Ever wonder why some people start a business but it never really gets off the ground? Don't get me wrong: I am 100% pro-entrepreneurship and I think if one has the right business model, they should go for it. Unfortunately, the statistics for long-term success are not in their favor.

I am sure you have a friend or family member who thought they had the right idea and would succeed. They refinanced their personal residence or borrowed money only to see their business fail. They lost everything and had to file for bankruptcy.

I understand the appeal of being your own boss. When you work for someone else, you are creating wealth for the person who owns the business. When you have your own business, you can build wealth for yourself.

When people decide to start their own business, they may not spend much time thinking about whether their business will stand out from similar businesses. This is one of the major reasons why businesses fail.

And even if their business is doing okay, they might be putting in ridiculous hours and sacrificing time with their loved ones to keep the business afloat. Do they really own their business, or does their business own them?

I think you know where I am going with this. By the time you finish reading this chapter, I hope you will agree with me that a real estate investment business is a much better option than a traditional small business.

First, let's consider why businesses fail

Is it true that more than half of new businesses fail during the first year? Not quite. The Small Business Administration (SBA) states that 30% of new businesses fail during their first two years, 50% during their first five years, and 66% during their first ten years.

According to Investopedia, the most common reasons why small businesses fail are (1) insufficient capital; (2) poor management; (3) inadequate business planning; and (4) spending so much on marketing that they have cash flow problems. But there are more than four reasons why early-stage businesses in the United States don't survive.

CBInsights identified the following reasons why small businesses fail:

42% lack a market need for their services or products

29% run out of cash

23% have poor management

19% are out-competed

18% have pricing and cost issues

17% have a poor product offering

17% lack a business model

14% have poor marketing

14% ignore their customers

Clearly, there are many reasons why small businesses fail, but a few keep coming to the top: insufficient capital, unpredictable cash flow, lack of demand, and poor management.

Just to make a point, let's look at the challenges you would face if you decided to open a new pizza restaurant. According to the "2018 Pizza Power Report: A State-of-the-Industry Analysis," a total of 4,992 new *pizzerias* opened their doors in the preceding year while 5,291 ***closed.***

The Perry Group International and the Restaurant Brokers studied the average lifespan of restaurants. The Perry Group study concluded that most restaurants close during their first year of operation. Seventy percent of those that make it past the first year close their doors within the next five years. Ninety percent of the restaurants that are still operating past the five-year mark will stay in business for a minimum of 10 years.

The Restaurant Brokers study, which was the only one to make a distinction between chain and independent restaurants, concluded that up to 90% of independent establishments close during the first year and the remaining restaurants have an average lifespan of five years.

Here are the hard numbers associated with opening a restaurant:

- ✓ Median cost to open a restaurant: **$275,000**
- ✓ Average low cost to open a restaurant: **$125,000**
- ✓ Average high cost to open a restaurant: **$555,000**
- ✓ Average cost (with a building): **$425,000**

I am guessing that when restaurants go out of business and the equipment has to be sold, the owners are lucky to get back 10 to 50 percent of the money they invested.

Visit any city in our country and in all likelihood you will see the same types of small businesses (gift shops, independent clothing stores, restaurants, bars, gyms, thrift stores, auto parts stores, auto repair shops, and so on). Do you know anyone who started one of these businesses and went broke? If you ever took a Business 101 class, you know this lesson by heart: You must differentiate your business to give customers a reason to choose you over the competition. It's likely that many similar types of businesses in your area operate in the same segment and target the same clientele. What makes your business model different? If it is very similar to your competitors, what makes you stand out?

The outlook for real estate investors is different

A real estate investment business is less likely to fail than a traditional business, but failure can happen if people make some (or all) of the following mistakes:

- ✓ *Not interviewing real estate agents to find an agent who is an investor* with the expertise to explain the advantages and disadvantages of various real estate options.

- ✓ *Buying low-quality properties in undesirable areas instead of purchasing worthwhile properties in family-friendly neighborhoods.* If you need money in an emergency, how easy will it be to sell a property in a high-crime area? Who would be the likely buyer?

- ✓ *Investing without knowing why they want to invest in the first place.* The "big why" for real estate investing should be to build wealth, retirement income, and financial freedom, not just cash flow with no goal in mind.

- ✓ *Not having a business plan and buying properties that don't fit their short- or long-range plans.* (A sample business plan is provided in Chapter 13.) Investors should buy enough of the right properties to provide cash flow, tax savings, appreciation, and depreciation now while gradually paying off the properties in order to build wealth for retirement.

- ✓ *Falling in love with the property rather than the deal* and not taking the time to analyze a property under consideration. Are you unsure whether property A, B, or C would be a good investment? Using some basic formulas (see Chapter 9) will help you make good choices.

- ✓ *Overleveraging properties by relying on low down payment or "no money down" deals.* If a deal seems too good to be true, it probably is. Why would anyone sell a property worth owning for no money down?

- ✓ *Constantly refinancing properties instead of paying them off.* I understand that refinancing is often necessary in the beginning so you can build a portfolio, but at some point your goal should be to pay them off. If you have little or no equity, you have no protection if anything goes wrong. Your age should also be a consideration in deciding how aggressive to be. Is it a good strategy to keep accumulating properties, or is it more important to own enough of the right properties that are paid off? Why would anyone who is nearing retirement age want to be aggressive and overleverage?

- ✓ *Collecting rent but not making the mortgage payment.* You may not believe anyone would do this, but I listed a few properties from a local bank where this actually happened. It is one of the main reasons some real estate investors fail.

- ✓ *Not maintaining the property.* Why would anyone invest their hard-earned money in a property and then allow it to become run-down?

- ✓ *Poor tenant screening through a lack of due diligence.* One example of poor tenant screening might be renting to someone who wants to pay cash for the first month's rent and security deposit. How many people with a legitimate source of income have a couple of thousand dollars of cash on hand?

- ✓ Not inspecting the property at least on a quarterly basis. Think about it. If the condition of the property during the first three months is not satisfactory to you, it is unlikely to improve and could end up costing you thousands in the end.

Why do I think a real estate investment business is a winner?

Anyone considering a new business venture should think long and hard regarding the kind of business that is likely to succeed over the long term.

With a solid business plan and enough of the right properties, I am confident that anyone who is willing to make the necessary sacrifices now will be rewarded later. Here are some of the reasons real estate investing makes more sense for most people than owning a traditional small business.

- ✓ Housing will always be a necessity, no matter what is happening with the economy.

- ✓ When you invest in real estate, it is virtually impossible to lose your entire investment even if you need to sell a property quickly. (Keep in mind that a savvy investor will always buy undervalued properties.)

✓ You can start a real estate investment business and operate it part-time while keeping your current job.

✓ Your rental properties will continue working for you 24/7 because the tenant keeps paying rent. By comparison, if there's a blizzard the business closes and the owner still must pay expenses.

✓ If you purchase residential properties in desirable areas, they will always be in demand and will appreciate in value.

✓ Overhead costs are virtually nonexistent because you can run a real estate business from your kitchen table using your smartphone and computer without hiring any employees.

✓ You can run the business alone until your portfolio has grown to the point where you might need help. Repairs on your properties are handled by independent contractors. Other members of your team (which could include your attorney, accountant, title company, termite inspector, home inspector, and so on) can be utilized as needed.

✓ A real estate business is resistant to inflation, because property values and rent usually increase during periods of inflation.

✓ When taxes, insurance, and expenses go up, you can raise the rent to cover those costs.

- ✓ Even if the real estate market goes south, savvy investors who purchase undervalued properties are well protected. If a property is used as a long-term rental, the tenant is making the mortgage payment.
- ✓ In addition to the long-term rental model, you have the option of wholesaling some of your properties to other investors or "flipping" them to buyers of owner-occupied properties. (Both options are covered in later chapters.)
- ✓ The 1031 tax-deferred exchange is available only to real estate investors. It allows you to sell a property for a profit and defer capital gains taxes in the year of the sale. You can use the 1031 exchange over and over as you grow your portfolio.
- ✓ As your rental properties are paid off, your net worth goes up. Depending on the size of your portfolio, becoming a millionaire is the real deal in a decade or two. I have a few clients that achieved at least $1,000,000 net worth in just 3 to 4 years.

I am living proof that real estate investing is one of the most lucrative businesses to start up today. Over the 45-plus years that I have been doing this, it has been an amazing journey with very little drama. I have created more wealth than I ever expected while helping many of my clients achieve financial freedom.

In my 45 years of being an investor, I can't recall anyone who applied solid business principles and owned properties in family-friendly neighborhoods and still went out of business. Additionally, the same applies to my clients. Think about it: Shelter has met the test of time, and it will always be a necessity and never go out of favor. Real estate is a winning proposition, and anyone willing to work hard can be successfully as long as they are creditworthy.

A record number of Americans are now millionaires

According to Spectrem Group's *Market Insights Report 2018*, the number of U.S. households reporting net worth between $1 million and $5 million, not including primary residence (NIPR), grew by nearly 600,000 in the previous year to nearly 10 million. This represents a 6.2% increase and is the largest year-to-year growth for this segment that has been reported since 2009. Sizable increases were also recorded across all other wealth segments.

Spectrem Group's annual report analyzes the number of wealthy households in America based on net worth, from the Mass Affluent ($100,000 minimum) to the $25-million-plus segment. The report also includes information on the investment habits and behaviors of investors based on advisor usage and occupation.

Key findings include:

- ✓ In 2017, there were 31 million Mass Affluent households with a net worth between $100,000 and $1 million NIPR. That is an increase of half a million households from 2016.
- ✓ The number of millionaires—those with a net worth between $1 million and $5 million—climbed to 9.98 million, an increase of almost 600,000 compared with 2016.
- ✓ The Ultra High Net Worth market, in which net worth is between $5 million and $25 million, grew to 1,348,000 households, an increase of 84,000 from 2016.

✓ There are now 172,000 households with a net worth exceeding $25 million. That reflects an increase of 16,000 households from the 2016 total, representing an increase of more than 10 percent from the 2016 total of 156,000.

"The combination of record financial market performance and accelerating economic growth in 2017 has continued to increase the population of affluent Americans," said George H. Walper Jr., president of Spectrem Group. "It is particularly notable that the number of $25-million-plus households has grown by more than 10 percent in one year. There are now 55,000 more $25-million-plus households in 2017 than there were just five years earlier in 2012."

My eight keys to becoming a millionaire real estate investor

1. Find a real estate agent who is a residential investment specialist and an investor with the expertise to guide you every step of the way.

2. Start your own real estate business. You will be glad you did.

3. Develop a business plan and evaluate it annually. (A sample business plan is provided in Chapter 13.)

4. Dream and think about how it would feel to be a millionaire. Buy a million dollars' worth of property using leverage. Own a million dollars after loans are paid off. (Steps: Think, Buy, and Own a Million).

5. Save, save, save until you have enough money for a down payment on a property. Then start over and buy another and another.

6. Live below your means. Before buying something, first ask yourself, "Do I really need this?"
7. Avoid using credit cards. (If you do use them, pay off the balances monthly.)
8. Let your money work hard for you so you won't have to work hard for your money. Buy assets that appreciate in value.

Even though we now have a record number of millionaires in the United States, the middle class is shrinking. The percentage of American adults who are considered middle-income fell from 55% in 2000 to 52% in 2014, according to a 2016 report from the Pew Research Center. In addition, many Americans are living paycheck to paycheck. One in three people surveyed said that they wouldn't be able to come up with $2,000 if faced with an emergency like an urgent home repair, medical crisis, or car accident. Even affluent two-income households reported feeling pinched.

How big is the demand for rental properties?

According to data collected by the National Association of Realtors, more than ten million Americans own rental properties. Investors accounted for 15% of residential transactions in 2017.

More people are renting than at any other point in the past 50 years. In 2016, 36.6% of household heads rented their home, close to the 1965 number of 37%, according to a report prepared by the Pew Research Center based on data from the Census Bureau. The total number of U.S. households had grown by 7.6 million over the past decade, Pew reported. However, the number of households headed by homeowners had remained relatively flat, while households headed by renters had grown by nearly 10% during the same time period.

Rising home prices, lingering fears from the housing crash, and large amounts of student debt are some of the reasons why many Americans see the appeal of renting. Millennials (age 35 and younger) are the age group most likely to rent, Pew found. In 2016, 65% of households headed by young adults were renting, up 8 percentage points from 2006.

Another reason for renting could be that young adults haven't accumulated enough wealth for a down payment on a house. Also, owning a home inhibits moving, and young adults are the most likely age group to move, so they may prefer not to own until their lives are more settled.

As you can see by the above statistics, the opportunity to build wealth by acquiring rental property is endless because housing will always be a necessity and will never go out of favor, unlike other types of small businesses that are less likely to survive.

Key points to remember:

- ✓ Fifty percent of small businesses fail before reaching the five-year mark.
- ✓ Starting a real estate investment business is less risky than starting a traditional small business because it is impossible to lose your entire investment in real estate.
- ✓ A crucial aspect of succeeding in real estate is buying undervalued properties in desirable areas.
- ✓ If you make the right choices, maintain your properties, and screen your tenants carefully, you can become a millionaire real estate investor.
- ✓ Real estate will always be a lucrative investment because the demand for housing will never disappear.

Chapter 4

REAL ESTATE VERSUS STOCKS

A recent survey asked the following question: "Which of the following do you think is the best long-term investment: bonds, real estate, savings accounts or CDs, stocks or mutual funds, or gold?" The graph shows the percentages of people who chose each category.

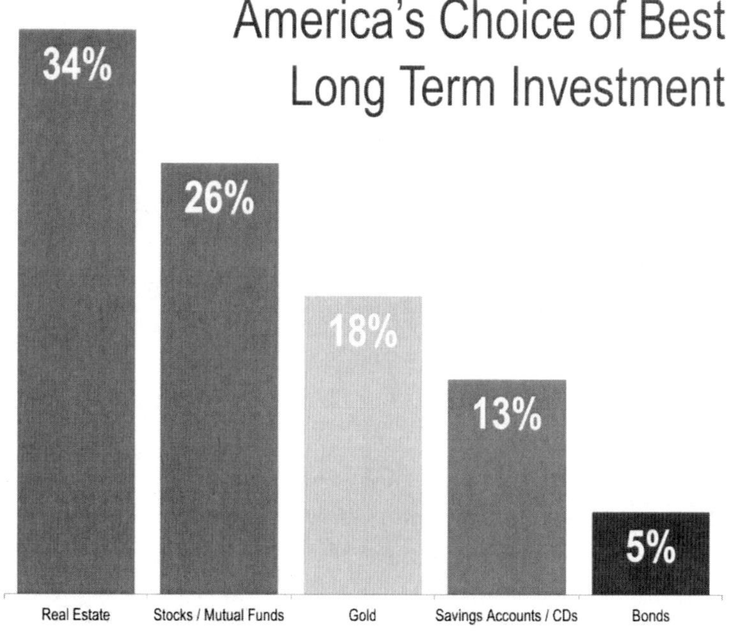

Real estate is the top-ranking investment among most subgroups of Americans across gender, age, and income categories—with a few notable exceptions. Young adults and residents of the East and Midwest are about equally likely to name stocks as real estate, and lower-income Americans' top choice is a tie between real estate and gold. The percentage who rank stocks as the best investment varies with household income, ranging from 19% among those earning less than $35,000 annually to 33% among those earning $75,000 or more.

For most people, real estate is a better investment than stocks

Now that the economy is on fire, all Americans should be rejoicing in their wealth, right? Wrong! Only 52% of Americans own any stocks at all, according to a recent Gallup poll. Are you part of the 52%?

According to the Federal Reserve, of the 10% of families with the highest incomes, 92% owned stocks as of 2013 (the latest year for their study), the same level of ownership as in 2007. But stock ownership decreased among people in the bottom half of the income distribution.

The top 10% of Americans owned an average of $969,000 in stocks. The next 40% owned $132,000 on average. For the bottom half of families, the average amount invested in the stock market was just under $54,000. With an increase of more than 200% in the S&P 500 since 2009, the wealth gap has clearly widened.

What is happening to the 48% of people who are not investing in the stock market? If you are part of that group, what has kept you from investing in the stock market? Is it fear of losing your hard-earned money? Is it because you don't have enough money to invest to make it worthwhile? Is it because you don't understand how the market works? If you don't understand the stock market, you are not alone. A majority of people have no clue either. I bet at some point you have thought about real estate because it is much easier to understand. My hope is that this book is giving you the knowledge to pull the trigger. With the right residential investment specialist on your side, becoming a millionaire doesn't have to be a dream but can become a reality. Real estate investment is a terrific alternative to stocks.

Rather than putting your money in the stock market, why not invest it in real estate? We can debate this subject all day long, but ultimately it comes down to your personal preferences. How much control do you want over your investments?

If you invest in the stock market, increasing the value of your investment is beyond your control. Investing in stocks is not a bad option if you want no involvement at all. Based on the conversations I have with my clients on a regular basis, hands down they prefer to be in control of their own financial future. That's why real estate is their preferred option.

I like my real estate business model much better than the stock market because it is easier for me to understand. When you buy an investment property you can see it, touch it, and make changes that increase its value. My business model is simple: Buy the right property, rent it to a qualified tenant, collect rent, make the mortgage payment, and maintain the property by making needed repairs or renovations. Bottom line: The money that is left over is mine to spend or invest as I want.

The following chart compares the benefits of real estate and stocks:

Offering	Real Estate	Stocks
Cash Flow (Dividends)	√	√
1031 Exchange	√	
Appreciation	√	√
Leverage	√	√
Tangible Asset	√	
Owner Control	√	
Principle Reduction	√	
Liquidity	√	√
Tax Benefits	√	

As you can see, real estate offers more to investors than stock does. Here's a brief rundown:

- ✓ If you own a rental property you receive monthly cash flow that you can spend. This cash flow from your real estate investment, which I will call "dividends," is the rental income minus expenses and after debt service (payments to the bank or other lender). With stocks, you can either reinvest the dividends or cash out and pay taxes on your profits.
- ✓ As a real estate investor you can defer your capital gains tax by using a powerful tool available only for real estate transactions: a 1031 tax-deferred exchange. When you sell your stocks and make a profit you cannot defer taxes on the profit.

✓ Both real estate and stocks can increase in value (appreciation), but housing will always be a necessity so its value is more stable during economic downturns.

✓ Real estate investors can use the power of leverage to increase their return on investment (ROI). To illustrate the power of leverage, let's consider two different real estate scenarios with different ROIs.

In Scenario 1 you put a 20% down payment on a $100,000 property. You are controlling an asset worth $100,000 by investing only $20,000. In other words, you are using other people's money to make the purchase. (*Note:* I am aware that the average price of a home in your community may be higher or lower than $100,000.)

If your property generates $13,200 in yearly income and requires $5,000 in expenses, you have $8,200 in net operating income (NOI). Your NOI must be high enough to cover debt service to the bank, which is the principal and interest (PI) on your mortgage. Let's say your annual PI is $5,000, leaving you with $3,200 as your cash flow before taxes. To determine your return on investment (ROI), divide $3,200 by the total amount of cash invested. Your $20,000 down payment plus closing costs of $2,000 equals a total investment of $22,000. Divide $3,200 by $22,000 and you have a ROI of 14.5%.

In Scenario 2 you pay $100,000 cash for the property. The $100,000 selling price plus $2,000 closing costs equals a total investment of $102,000. You are not making any mortgage payments in this scenario, so your ROI is $8,200 (NOI) / $102,000 (Total Investment) = 8.0%. See why I recommend using the power of leverage by making a down payment instead of paying cash for a property?

By contrast with both of the above scenarios, let's say you decide to invest $20,000 in the stock market. If your stock goes up 5% annually, the value of your stock investment increases by $1,000 per year. How much of that $1,000 are you able to spend without selling the stock? *None of it.*

Could you buy $100,000 worth of stocks with $20,000? Yes. Buying on *margin involves* borrowing money from a broker to purchase *stock*. You *can* think of it as a loan from your brokerage that allows you to buy more *stock* than you normally could. To trade on *margin*, you need a *margin* account. Buying *stock* on *margin* is only profitable *if* your *stocks go* up enough to pay back the loan *with* interest. If the value of your stocks drops too much, you will lose your principal and then some. When this strategy is used wisely and prudently, it can be a valuable tool. Margin is primarily used by high-net-worth individuals.

✓ Real estate is a tangible asset that you can see and touch, but stocks are not. That's why I believe real estate is easier to understand than stocks.

✓ When you invest in real estate, you can make changes that increase the value of your property (owner control). When you invest in stocks, there is absolutely nothing you can do personally to increase their value.

✓ When you purchase a property and rent it out, the tenant is helping you make your mortgage payment and the principal amount is reduced accordingly each month. Of course, it's not good to have principal reduction with stocks because it means you are losing money. Unfortunately, it happens quite often.

- ✓ Liquidity is commonly offered as proof that stocks are a better investment than real estate. I have sold houses that closed in one week. If it had taken two to three weeks to close the sale, it wouldn't have been a big inconvenience for anybody. With stocks, you can receive your money in two to four days. This comparison does not convince me that stock is a better investment than real estate.
- ✓ When you purchase real estate, you get tax benefits such as depreciation and deductions. When you buy stocks, you only get a tax break if you lose money on your investment; otherwise, Uncle Sam gets his cut in the form of taxes.

That gives you my take on why I believe real estate is a far better investment than stocks, especially for the average hard-working American who has about $20,000 to invest. When the property is paid off, not only have you been receiving rent every month, but you have an asset that likely is worth a lot more than you originally paid for it.

Did you know that most stocks and bonds in this country are held by a small minority of the U.S. population, and most of the stocks are owned by the wealthiest 1%?

Is the money you have invested in the market significant enough to allow you to maintain your current lifestyle in retirement?

Would you be able to live off your investments if you could no longer make a living from what you are doing now?

How does real estate compare with other investments?

Of all the investments that are within the reach of the average individual, no other investment offers the full range of benefits that are available to real estate investors. Investments such as stocks, bonds, savings accounts, mutual funds, and CDs have pros and cons when it comes to "risk versus return." For comparison purposes, let's look at one more scenario that illustrates why investing in real estate is much better for most people than investing in stocks.

Let's say you have $50,000 to invest in either stocks or real estate. You could buy $50,000 worth of stocks or use the same amount of money to make a 20% down payment on real estate that has a total value of $250,000. Depending on your area, you might be able to purchase several properties that generate income. Keep in mind that investors generally buy properties that are good deals (priced 20% to 40% below what they sold for a few years ago). If you are able to find some good deals, your initial $50,000 could be controlling much more than $250,000 because the properties are worth more than their purchase price.

If the value of your stocks or real estate went up by, say, 10%, then your stocks would be worth $55,000, giving you $5,000 profit. But your real estate would be worth $275,000, giving you $25,000 profit. That's a 50% return on your initial investment of $50,000.

How much control do you have over the future value of your $50,000 worth of stock? None. By contrast, could you do anything that might increase the value of your $250,000 worth of property? Since your properties are undervalued, they may need a little cosmetic work, such as paint, landscaping, new bathroom fixtures, or updated kitchen appliances. There are lots of things you can do to improve a property without spending a lot of money.

Now let's assume your stock does well and the shares you purchased double in value. Your $50,000 in stock is now worth $100,000. What can you do with the equity? Just one thing: sell your stock. Of course, that will create capital gains tax liability and reduce the amount that is to invest now or in the future.

By contrast, let's say a few years go by and your $250,000 property is now worth $500,000. What can you do to take advantage of the equity? You could sell the property, but that may not be the smartest option. Keep in mind the benefits your rental property is providing in the form of cash flow, appreciation, tax advantages, and principal reduction, to name a few. Why would anyone want to sell a property that is increasing in value and generating income at the same time? What's more, if you did sell it, you would have to pay capital gains tax on the profit.

A better option to take advantage of the equity would be to refinance the property or do a 1031 tax-deferred exchange. The money would not be taxable if you used it to purchase additional investment properties.

Or how about this scenario: let's say you go back to your bank and ask for an 80% loan-to-value mortgage of $400,000. After paying off your original $200,000 loan, you would still have $200,000 that could be used as down payments (at 20% of the purchase price) to purchase more properties. That amount would give you $1,000,000 in purchasing power. The property you purchased initially is now worth $500,000 and you have acquired additional property worth $1,000,000 for a combined real estate portfolio of $1,500,000.

Can you now see the power of investing in real estate compared to stocks? This is the power of leverage hard at work. To simplify this explanation the amount of principal reduction was not taken into consideration, but it would have made the scenario even better.

Clearly, real estate is head and shoulders above any other investment. Imagine giving your stockbroker the following instructions:

"I would like to buy some stock, but I can only pay 20% down. I would like the stock to go up in value over time and pay dividends. When the stock goes up, I may want to pull tax-free cash out of it and keep the stock. At some point, I may also want to sell it and pay no taxes and then buy other stocks with the profit from the sale. Oh, and by the way, I would also like a tax deduction every year as long as I own this stock for the next 27½ years." (*Note:* A residential property can be depreciated for tax purposes for 27½ years and a commercial property for 39 years.)

What do you think your broker's reaction would be? He or she would probably laugh out loud, thinking you were making a joke.

Over the 45-plus years I have been investing in real estate, I have enjoyed having a high level of control over my investments. I can take steps to improve my property and increase the income it generates. By contrast, I lost most of the money I invested in the stock market because I did not understand it and had to rely on my broker for advice. I even had to pay a commission to sell the stuff. But with real estate, my investment will always be worth something.

Do you know anyone who makes at least $200 per month in dividends from their current investments other than real estate? As a real estate investor, you can do this with just one rental (cash flow). If you own multiple properties, you can generate much more cash flow while your tenants pay down your debt. With a good credit history, hard-working people from all walks of life can benefit from real estate investing. I have personally witnessed many people become millionaires with this type of business. If you choose properties wisely and follow the advice in this book, you can build a sizable portfolio that generates a six-figure annual income. How many people do you know who are earning this much from their stock or other investment options that offers as many tax benefits as real estate?

Key points to remember:

- ✓ Real estate investors can increase the value of their investment property, but stock market investors have no control over the value of their stock.
- ✓ Real estate gives you the power of leverage, allowing you to earn a higher return on your investment than you could get in the stock market.
- ✓ If you hold onto properties and rent them out, you receive cash from your tenants each month. When you invest in stock, you receive no cash until you sell your shares.
- ✓ When you sell an investment property, you can use the 1031 exchange to defer capital gains taxes on your profits. You also have many other tax breaks that are not available to stock market investors.

Chapter 5

WHAT TO LOOK FOR IN A RESIDENTIAL REAL ESTATE INVESTMENT SPECIALIST

When you decide to invest in real estate, your first step should be finding a real estate agent who can serve as your coach, mentor, consultant, and wealth advisor. Your agent should always have your best interests in mind.

Is the agent that helped you purchase your personal resident qualified to help you succeed as an investor? Maybe not. If somebody asked your agent what they do for a living, what would they say? Giving an answer like "I help people from all walks of life buy and sell houses" is not good enough, because any licensed real estate agent is qualified to represent buyers and sellers in a transaction. If you are looking to invest in real estate, you need to choose an agent who can truthfully say: "I represent people who buy and sell houses, but I am also an investor and investment specialist, and I help people generate wealth and retirement income. In other words, I mentor, coach, and serve as a consultant and wealth advisor to my clients." When you get this type of response from an agent that you like and trust, you have found the right person to work with.

My idea of an investor-friendly real estate agent is one who sees things others don't see… one who has an eye for an opportunity and is excellent at spotting "the deal."

Here's another way to put it. Real estate agents have different credentials, just as doctors do. If you had a problem with your heart, you would make an appointment with a cardiologist, not an oncologist or gynecologist. Would you be interested in your cardiologist's training and credentials? The same should apply to the real estate industry. Does the agent under consideration have the credentials you are looking for?

What should you expect from your agent?

If you intend to invest in real estate, your expectations for an agent should be different from the expectations of someone who wants to buy or sell a personal residence.

To bring added value to you as a real estate investor, your agent should:

- ✓ Know and understand your goals.
- ✓ Have a basic understanding of tax considerations.
- ✓ Understand the pros and cons of different types of investments.
- ✓ Be able to analyze a property to determine whether it will be a good investment.
- ✓ Control a sizable real estate portfolio.
- ✓ Have experience flipping properties.
- ✓ Be able to explain the advantages and disadvantages of the real estate investment choices that are available to a potential investor.
- ✓ Understand 1031 exchanges and 401(K), self-directed, and Roth IRAs.

- ✓ Be familiar with local property values and comparables.
- ✓ Know how to search the MLS for deals.
- ✓ Maintain relationships with local banks, lenders, and others who deal with investors.
- ✓ Know the landlord/tenant laws of your state (http://www.thelpa.com/lpa/lllaw.html).

Bottom line: To serve as your real estate consultant or wealth advisor, your agent must be able to provide services that other real estate agents do not offer. Their skills should set them apart from other real estate agents who lack this knowledge. You should feel confident that they are the missing piece of the puzzle. They should be able to help you every step of the way to ensure that you will accomplish your objectives.

Very simply put, keep in mind that a real estate license gives an agent the opportunity to represent buyers and sellers in a real estate transaction in exchange for a commission. Unless an agent has specialized training in this "niche market," you would be making a big mistake if you decided to work with them simply because you like and trust them. If they lack knowledge about investing in real estate, you probably should not be using them.

Unless they are an investor or they took an investment class, their real estate training did not prepare them to work with investors. Most real estate agents lack this knowledge, and maybe that is why more are not aware that real estate is one of the best investment options to generate wealth.

If your current agent doesn't work with real estate investors, ask them who they recommend or contact the brokers of the top two or three real estate agencies in your community and ask them to recommend an agent who has the knowledge you are looking for. The top producer in the agency is not necessarily the right person to work with unless they own rental properties and work with investors.

If the top producer has the investment credentials, talk to them. However, they may be a rock star agent but not own even one rental property. This is of no help to you. What you want to know is whether they are working with investors on a regular basis and how many investment properties they have sold. If they don't have the experience and knowledge to help you, find someone who does.

I don't know how many agents in your community would fit this description, but I am sure you will find the right one. Some, like myself, make a terrific living by helping clients build wealth and retirement income, but they also do their fair share of business with buyers and sellers of owner-occupied properties. I bring added value as I am an active investor who understands the ins and outs of this business. I have flipped a lot of houses, so I practice what I am recommending that others should do.

With all the benefits that real estate offers, I was surprised to read in an industry publication recently that less than 3% of real estate agents own at least one investment property. That percentage is shockingly low. Why more agents don't invest in their own industry is beyond me. They know values, areas, comparables and what is considered to be a good deal or not. So why aren't more agents investing in their own industry? Maybe because they have the same fears and lack of knowledge as others who are not getting in the game.

There is a big difference about giving advice about real estate and giving advice about investing in real estate.

Real estate experts are in high demand

If you are fortunate to find a real estate agent who meets your criteria, they will be highly sought after. Please don't take it personally if they don't immediately agree to work with you. Prior to establishing a relationship with you, they must gather enough information to see whether you will be a good fit for them. On the other hand, you also need to take time to determine whether you want to do business with a specific agent.

As you know, not every person who wants to invest in real estate has the right motives or the financial wherewithal to get started. This business is not about get-rich-quick schemes or empty promises. It's about building a long-term relationship with your agent and following a business plan that will build wealth and retirement income.

You want your agent to take you seriously so they will dedicate some of their time and energy to you. I am certain that in your own line of work you want to do business only with people of integrity who are loyal and trustworthy, and you also want to know something about them before doing business with them. Your real estate agent feels the same way about potential clients. To help you prepare for your first meeting, this chapter includes a list of suggested questions to ask the agent.

Agents should be an advocate for their industry

Real estate agents make a living by helping clients buy and sell their personal residences, but they can generate wealth by investing in real estate and helping their clients do the same. Here's the bottom line: If your agent does not own real estate, it is highly unlikely they will able to provide the guidance that will help you be successful as a real estate investor.

When agents understand that working with people like you can be one of the most important aspects of their business, it's a win-win for them and for you. When they help you accomplish your goals, you are more likely to tell others how good they are. When they help people like you they will make more money they ever realized they could, so they will not need to be concerned about commission checks.

Why should a real estate investment specialist want to work with you?

For an agent, working with investors is like cultivating a garden and watching it grow.

Since I got my license in 1998, I have sold a lot of properties for my clients and bought and sold a fair amount of my own properties. I continue to do a fair amount of business, yet I don't consider myself to be any better than other agents.

My business hasn't grown as a result of doing phone duty or through luck but rather because I am an investor with the credentials to help clients generate wealth. I have the mindset of an investor instead of a real estate agent and the agent that you work with should feel the same way. It is much easier to gain credibility with investors when you can proudly say you are an investor. If someone asks me whether I own any rentals or have flipped a property, I can enthusiastically say "Yes."

There are many agents in every real estate company who work hard and are knowledgeable and experienced but are struggling to make a living. They don't do a lot of business and are always looking for more clients. I can't help but wonder why they are missing out on potential income by overlooking clients who need help to solve their financial concerns and are investors.

Why would an agent choose to work with investors?

First and foremost, investors have great potential for repeat business. Many times, owner-occupied buyers won't even remember their agent's name the next time they decide to list their home. A buyer of owner-occupied property may utilize their agent's services every five to seven years at most, while investors will use an agent over and over if the agent can bring them deals that make sense. Not only will the agent earn a commission when an investor buys a property that they intend to flip, but also when the client sells it.

One of the most rewarding referrals I ever received began working with me in 2005. That same client has purchased more than 300 properties in the past thirteen years. One year he made $300,000 by flipping properties.

From an agent's point of view, investors also are easier to work with than owner-occupied home buyers and are not as demanding. In my experience, investors are not as emotional as home buyers. Many times, they will write an offer right on the spot. A 10-minute showing can result in an accepted offer.

Investors also are not as concerned about minor cosmetic details as home buyers are. Their focus is on the financial numbers and whether they can make money from their investment by flipping it or holding it as a long-term rental.

Working with investors is not only financially rewarding but also deeply satisfying to me. When I have earned their trust, they will listen to my advice and be grateful because I am helping them make a good living and build wealth. Often I am bringing them more value than their financial planner or stockbroker does. I don't have to negotiate my commission because my clients know that I have helped them make money.

How to build a mutually rewarding relationship with your agent

Keep in mind that your chosen agent has knowledge and expertise that is extremely valuable, so it is important to listen to their advice. You must be reasonable with your expectations as well. If your agent has a busy practice, their time is valuable so be sure to use it wisely. Don't waste it by asking them to write unrealistic offers that are unlikely to materialize.

If you pick the right agent, that person will be the fastest path to accomplish your objectives. You should see them as your mentor, coach, or wealth builder.

They should know the neighborhoods in your city, be familiar with property values, and know where to find an undervalued property. Loyalty is very important to them and it should be to you as well. If they have a good client base their challenge is to decide which client to call first when they find out about a great deal.

When you become an investor, a knowledgeable agent is the most important member of your team. (The roles of other members of the team will be discussed in later chapters.)

Here are some points to keep in mind. Your agent should:

1. Be knowledgeable. It helps if they are also an investor (even on a small scale) because it means they have personal experience with the investment process.

2. Be comfortable writing multiple offers while also being aware that writing low-ball offers is often a waste of time for everyone involved.

3. Have some experience helping others like you. You should have the confidence that you are in good hands. Keep in mind that this is not playtime as you will perhaps be making your biggest financial investments ever.

4. Have a good reputation for helping investors make money. Success breeds success. When they do a good job for you, you'll be more likely to refer them to your friends and others. Most of my clients have come to me through referrals.

5. Be honest with you. I would rather lose a deal than not tell the truth. Your agent must be able to put themselves in your shoes when you are evaluating a potential deal. They should be able to tell you if a property makes sense for you financially.

6. Behave with integrity and do the right thing instead of focusing on the next commission check.

7. Be able to find properties that meet your needs and objectives. For example, cash flow is more important to some buyers than to others.

8. Understand what you are looking for. Most investors will write offers with the same terms each time, such as cash, close in a short time, contractor/inspector contingency.

9. Not waste your time by telling you about properties that don't meet your criteria.

10. Have some knowledge regarding your local investors' or property owners' association.

11. Meet with you at least annually to find out whether your properties are still meeting your needs and review your business plan to make sure you are on track to accomplish your short- and long-term objectives.

12. Stay in touch with you and send you articles of interest and be the ongoing source for all your real estate investment needs.

13. Suggest sources of financing. Recommend banks that are friendly and are willing to loan money on investment properties with favorable terms. In my experience, local or community banks are much easier to work with than nationwide banks such as US Bank, Bank of the West, or Wells Fargo.

14. Provide information that will help you decide whether an undervalued property is a good deal.

15. Provide an estimate of the potential rent for the property under consideration.

16. Recommend lawyers who specialize in real estate, as well as accountants, contractors, and property managers.

17. Be prepared to handle a multitude of details after the offer has been accepted (such as contractor inspections, home inspections, termite inspections, and surveys).

18. Provide information about what is going on in the real estate marketplace, including neighborhoods that may be improving or declining.

19. Suggest things you can do to increase the value of your property, such as updating kitchens and baths.

When you find the right agent to work with, they will become a trusted partner and the missing piece of the puzzle for you. Once they are familiar with your needs, desires, short- and long-term objectives, you can expect to have a long and meaningful relationship. *The agent who is working with you should become irreplaceable.*

In advising you, your agent should always keep your best interests in mind. If they are too excited, aggressive, or desperate they could push you to make bad decisions. If they are too conservative, you could miss an opportunity. Remember that it's your money and not theirs, so they should not use the word "we" unless they have a vested interest in a transaction. Saying "my client" is much better than saying "we" when discussing a potential deal.

Ideally, your agent will be someone who can meet your needs as well as someone you like and trust. Although you may be tempted to "go it alone," the right agent can help you reach your destination much faster.

In Omaha, Nebraska, where most of my rentals are located, a 2-bedroom property generally rents for $800 to $950 and a 3-bedroom for approximately $900 to $1,100 or more depending on the area. If the property is close to a university, medical school, or law school, the rent may be much higher. As an example, I own a 4-bedroom, 2-bath property close to a medical school that rents for $1,300 and up.

I am aware that in your community the property values may be so high that the rent will not even cover the mortgage payment. If this is true for you, you might want to consider investing in other states where property values are more reasonable and your return on your investment will make it worthwhile. The best places to buy rental properties generally have three things in common: job growth, population growth, and affordability. As an example, the metro area of Omaha, Nebraska, is a very desirable area because of reasonable property values. It is a very favorable destination for investors from Colorado, California, and other states. This information is readily available on websites like these:

www.realwealthnetwork.com/learn/ bestplacestobuyrentalproperty

www.landlordology.com

Of course, if you choose to invest out of state you will need to find a real estate agent who will have your back and be able to recommend a property manager and others. Contact the broker of the top two or three real estate companies in your target community and ask them to recommend an agent who has the expertise you are looking for.

Sample questions to ask before working with an agent

Here is a list of sample questions to ask agents you are interviewing. Their answers will help you decide whether they are the right agent for your team. Keep in mind that the agents you talk with will also be very interested in your background and readiness level, so they will be asking you pertinent questions as well.

✓ How long have you been an agent, and how long have you been working with investors?

✓ Do you own any rental properties? If so, what type of property do you prefer (houses, duplexes, apartments, commercial etc.), and what has been your overall experience so far?

✓ How many investors are you currently working with?

✓ Are you working with any investors who have flipped houses? Have you flipped any houses yourself?

✓ How many investment properties have you sold in the past? What types of properties have you sold?

✓ What types of multi-units have you sold?

✓ Do you have any knowledge of the commercial real estate market?

✓ Do you know any bankers or lenders who are familiar with investment properties?

✓ Do you have a list of contractors that you could recommend?

✓ Would you provide me with contact information for some of your clients?

- ✓ In your opinion, what are the advantages and disadvantages of investing in houses, duplexes, and apartment buildings?

Hopefully, their responses to your questions will give you the confidence that you have found the right agent and you will be in very good hands with them.

You need to find an agent who specializes in the type of property that you prefer. For example, my niche is single-family homes, duplexes, and small apartment buildings.

First-hand experience as an investor speaks volumes. Keep in mind that even if you like and trust the agent who represented you in the sale of your personal property, they may not be the right person to help you succeed as an investor. If you decide to work with an agent who lacks experience with investors but they have your best interests in mind, they may offer to team up with an agent who works with investors.

In conclusion, my advice to you is to be loyal to your agent and to use them exclusively. Why should they be loyal to you and call you about that good deal if you are not loyal to them?

Key points to remember:

- ✓ Not everyone who has a real estate license is qualified to work with investors.
- ✓ If you intend to invest in real estate, your agent should have firsthand experience as an investor.
- ✓ Your agent should have your best interests in mind, because your success is their success.
- ✓ You deserve to hire an agent who knows more than you do.

Chapter 6

DO YOU HAVE WHAT IT TAKES TO SUCCEED AS AN INVESTOR?

At this point I am sure you have read enough about being an investor to know that there's much more involved than simply buying a property and collecting rent.

Unfortunately, some people think cash flow is the name of the game and they don't pay attention to things such as location and buying properties in family-friendly neighborhoods. Yes, cash flow is very important, but controlling enough of the right properties and then owning them free and clear should be your goal. Always keep in mind why you want to do this in the first place: to build wealth, retirement income, and financial freedom.

If a property is not located in a family-friendly neighborhood, will it accomplish your objectives? It may be the wrong choice, but you will have to be the judge.

Think about who will be the likely tenant if you buy a property in an unfavorable neighborhood. What are the chances the property will be rented by the same person for a long time? If cash flow is your main objective and you pay no attention to the image you want to maintain in your community by owning the right properties, your choices could cause your business to fail.

If you want to become an investor, let's consider the kinds of activities you will face on a regular basis. Keep in mind that real estate investment is a business. If your answer to some of the following questions is "No," your best strategy may be to hire a property manager. They are to real estate as your financial advisor is to your investment portfolio.

- ✓ Do you generally deal well with people? This is a "people" business and while the tenant is not your friend, being friendly and consistent is key. Just because they are the renter and you are the landlord doesn't mean you don't need to treat them with respect.
- ✓ Are you well organized and good at record keeping? If not, it will cost you dearly at tax time.
- ✓ Are you good at multi-tasking?
- ✓ Does taking a risk concern you? Keep in mind that it is much riskier to start a small business or to invest in the stock market where you can lose all your money. It is next to impossible to lose your total investment in real estate. With proper due diligence, the risk is minimal. Remember that wealth is found on the other side of risk.
- ✓ Are you willing to invest the time required to succeed in this business?
- ✓ Are you willing to make sacrifices today so you will be rewarded later?
- ✓ Are you handy with home improvement projects and willing to do some of the work yourself?
- ✓ Can you pay if need be for someone to do the work you are unable to do?
- ✓ Would you be able to evict a family for nonpayment of rent?

Always keep in mind that a lot of people have opinions about real estate and they may not have a clue why they are doing this. I would encourage you to listen to people that you respect and value who have been investors for a long time, but ultimately remember this is your money.

The most important question is "Do you have the makeup and personality to succeed in this business?" Real estate investing is not a get-rich-quick gimmick. If you have a realistic business plan and follow it, becoming a millionaire real estate investor is within your reach. Over the long haul, it will be a very rewarding business venture for you, as it has been for me as well as many of my clients.

Not every home buyer should become a real estate investor

As you know, real estate investors are also home buyers (because we all need to live someplace), but not all home buyers are real estate investors. My philosophy regarding one's personal residence is that it should also be considered an investment. Did you know that if you live in your personal residence for at least two years and then sell it, the profits from the sale are tax-free? I have done this quite a few times and then used the profit to buy more rental properties. A single person can make up to $250,000 and a married couple up to $500,000. What a great way to generate funds to buy more rental properties. Think about how many properties you can buy using the power of leverage.

Real estate investors purchase various kinds of real estate, ranging from single-family homes, duplexes, and apartments to commercial properties, land, and industrial parks. Upwards of 90% of my clients are real estate investors who prefer single-family homes, duplexes, small apartments, and some commercial properties. Single-family homes are much easier to sell, and often the buyer is a first-time homeowner.

For other types of investment properties, the buyer will likely be another investor. I am sure you can foresee how difficult it might be for two investors to agree. The seller thinks the property is worth much more and the buyer thinks the opposite.

Investors who want to succeed in this business must make sacrifices to be successful, and those who are not successful tend to be less disciplined and less willing to work hard to reach their goals. Most successful investors start out making sacrifices. They do much of the work on their properties with the goal of someday having a portfolio worth owning.

In my experience, few investors are interested in buying run-down properties in undesirable areas. Instead, they gravitate to family-friendly neighborhoods with properties that can be reconditioned to rent or flip. They take tremendous pride in the portfolio they own.

What is the difference between active and passive investors?

Investors may actively or passively invest in real estate. Active investors are those who make their own repairs or hire contractors. In other words, they are involved in this business on a regular basis.

By contrast, a passive investor is someone who does not want the day-to-day involvement and instead pays a property management company to handle maintenance, repairs, rent collection, and so on.

When I talk to people about the benefits of investing in real estate, some of them tell me "I am too busy" or "I don't have time to do that." It is true that being an active investor takes time and effort, but the rewards are well worth the sacrifices. For those who have the financial wherewithal to purchase property but not the time and energy to handle the day-to-day responsibilities of property ownership, being a passive investor is a good alternative.

Successful versus unsuccessful investors

In my 45-plus years as a real estate investor, I have encountered hundreds of investors. My investment clients range from contractors to doctors and everyone in between. I have worked with investors at every level of experience, from beginners to veterans. I even have a few clients who are real estate agents.

I've paid attention to the reasons why some of my fellow investors are successful while others are not. By "successful" I don't mean that they necessarily own a lot of properties but that they take a sensible approach to investing in real estate.

Based on my experience, here are the top ten characteristics of successful real estate investors:

1. They are not emotional in their buying decisions. Unlike home buyers, they will not buy a property simply because they fell in love with it. Rather, they always have a logical reason for buying a property. They might intend to purchase it as a long-term rental, to flip it (fix up and sell), or (if the deal is good enough) to wholesale the property "as is" to another investor and make a quick profit.

2. They minimize their exposure to risk by making calculated decisions and utilizing analytical tools to determine whether an investment is a good deal and worth buying.

3. Their primary objective is to benefit from the long-term wealth-building opportunities that real estate offers, not to get rich quickly.

4. They utilize strategies that reflect their objectives and their risk tolerance.

5. They make the necessary sacrifices to accomplish their objectives, and they are 100% dedicated to reaching their investment goals.

6. They will not overpay for a property, and they often write multiple offers.

7. They have a system in place, and they stick to it even if they encounter disappointments.

8. They know what they will buy and what they will walk away from.

9. They don't waste a lot of time analyzing a property before it is under contract.

10. They don't leave things to chance; instead, they treat each investment as a business venture.

By contrast, I have met several individuals who thought of themselves as investors but had portfolios that didn't make sense. They either paid too much for their properties or purchased properties with inadequate cash flow. Most of the blame for these errors belongs to the real estate agents who helped them, because the basic principles of real estate investment were not followed. It would be interesting to find out what goals these individuals had for their properties and how they selected the real estate agents who assisted them. Following my simple rule "Fall in love with the deal and not the property" will go a long way toward ensuring your success.

What do investors care about most?

Based on my experience, real estate investors focus on the following things in deciding whether to bid on a property: purchase price, cash flow, opportunity to build wealth and generate retirement income, and financing terms.

1. Wealth building and retirement income

The main reason to invest in real estate is to build wealth and create retirement income. Real estate can yield higher returns than the stock market or other investment options. It also is more stable and provides a hedge against inflation

2. Purchase price (finding good deals)

Many real estate agents struggle with the fact that investors like to write low-ball offers—maybe as low as 30% to 40% below asking price—but those days are gone. Yes, you can still find deals, but offers must be realistic, and you should always keep in mind the "Big Why." As an example, paying a few thousand dollars more may be the smartest strategy because in the long run the tenant is covering the payment anyway. Investors don't want to compete with home buyers and prefer to buy a property that is not suitable for home buyers because of the amount of work that will be required to fix it up. Because of the low inventory, these types of properties are not as easy to find, making it even more important to have the right real estate agent on your team. When you make an offer, it is important to know what you intend to do with the property. Do you want to flip it or hold it as a long-term rental? You will find more details on this topic in Chapter 10, "Flip or Hold?"

3. Cash flow

Very simply put, you need to figure out whether a property will give you enough cash flow after you pay the bills such as loan payments to the bank. How much cash flow is worthwhile? It depends on whether you need money today or are more concerned about having the tenant ultimately pay off the mortgage.

4. Financing terms

Most of the investors I work with purchase properties by paying cash (using a savings account or a line of credit, for example). They make the necessary improvements to increase the property's value and ultimately refinance and pull out most of their initial investment. They pay off the line of credit and start over with the next property. This model works every time. Having good credit is the key. The types of properties that are conducive to using this strategy over and over include foreclosures, estate sales, properties that need work and can be improved, and properties that have been listed for months or are vacant. Regardless of who the seller is, cash speaks volumes because no financing contingencies or appraisals are required, there's very little hassle, and the sale can close much sooner—sometimes in as little as one week. Of course, a conventional loan with a 20% to 25% down payment also can be used, but in a tight market such as we are currently in, this type of financing cannot compete with a cash offer even if it the cash offer is less than conventional financing.

Are you aware that you can purchase real estate with your 401K, Roth, or self-directed IRA? We will cover all of these options in Chapter 7, "How to Finance Your Investment Properties." If you are already an investor, you are likely familiar with a 1031 exchange. If not, this topic also is covered in Chapter 7.

How much experience do you have as a real estate investor?

- ✓ Do you currently own any rental properties? If so, what kinds of properties do you own (houses, duplexes, apartments, land, strip malls)?
- ✓ Do you have a background in business, real estate, or finance?
- ✓ Why do you think you may want to invest?
- ✓ Where does most of your knowledge come from? Is it from attending a hype-filled free seminar where the speaker made a lot of promises but provided little substance, leaving you more confused than you were before you attended?

What are your short-term and long-term objectives?

You should consider your age when you set your objectives. If you are in your thirties or forties, your goals are likely to be different from the goals of an investor who expects to retire within the next ten or fifteen years.

What kinds of properties are you interested in purchasing?

Your business plan should be your road map. Are you interested in flipping, buy-and-hold, or wholesaling? Do you want to buy single-family homes, multi-units, or commercial properties? What areas, neighborhoods, and communities appeal to you?

Are you creditworthy?

You should not even think about investing in real estate if your credit score is poor. Do you have a line of credit, access to cash, a solid financial statement or a working relationship with a bank? If the answer is "Yes," you are well on your way.

Are you looking for deals for yourself or for someone else?

A "bird dog" is someone who scouts properties for potential investors and gets paid a referral fee if the investor buys the property. Many real estate agents (myself included) feel that dealing with a bird dog is a waste of time because the bird dog is not the decision maker. I want to deal with the decision maker.

Are you the decision maker?

Are you buying alone or in a partnership? If you are not the sole decision maker and others are involved, your agent will want to show properties to you and your partners at the same time, not to each of you separately. If a property is a good deal, it is likely to sell quickly.

Successful investors have developed good habits

My story may not be any different from yours. Becoming a successful investor required me to make sacrifices. When I had a full-time job working 50 to 60 hours a week as an executive with the Boy Scouts of America, I made repairs on my investment properties on the weekends. I did just about everything except major electrical work, plumbing, and roof replacement.

When I became a successful real estate agent with a busy practice, however, I decided that my time would be better spent if I hired a property management company to take care of my rentals so I could free up more time to work with investors.

I consider myself to be an ordinary, street-savvy person, and working hard has never been a problem for me. I believe there is no replacement for hard work, and I have been willing to pay the price to achieve success.

I didn't have any wealthy role models in the real estate business, yet I knew quite a few friends and acquaintances who had managed to accumulate wealth. Some were lucky enough to have a family business, while others were CEOs and so on.

Subconsciously I probably thought about what those individuals had that I didn't. Were they smarter than I was? Did they work any harder than I did? Did they have more drive or ambition than I had? Everything about me indicated that I was a high achiever and a hard worker, so I began to believe that I too could someday become financially independent.

Along the way, I developed some habits that have served me well as an investor. First, I learned to set achievable goals. I think that everything worthwhile should have measurable goals. Creating a business plan will provide you with a way to measure your success.

My goal was to become a millionaire real estate investor. I achieved that goal several years ago.

Investors should have a goal of controlling a certain amount of the right type of real estate in family-friendly areas to ultimately replace their income from the workplace and allow them to maintain or improve their lifestyle in retirement. A million dollars' worth of real estate is not that difficult to control if you are creditworthy. Depending on the area where you live, that could include different combinations of properties. In my community, it could be in the form of twenty $50,000 properties or ten $100,000 properties. If your properties are well maintained and continuously occupied, within 15 to 20 years these properties will be paid in full.

After your properties are paid in full, you will have substantial cash flow. As an example, let's say you have ten $100,000 properties that average $1,000 each in monthly income after subtracting expenses. Your properties will generate a total of $10,000 per month or $120,000 annually less expenses (taxes, insurance, maintenance, and so on).

There are many ways to become a millionaire real estate investor, and that is why real estate is such a powerful opportunity for the average hard-working individual. It's next to impossible to become a millionaire by working for someone else.

Becoming a millionaire real estate investor seemed like a distant dream to me at the beginning of my career, but aiming for that lofty goal gave me the drive and determination to make steady progress toward my objective.

As I look back over my real estate career, it is clear that the most successful investors take the time and effort to write a business plan and then follow it. I also have seen the mistakes made by people who didn't treat real estate as a business. If you want to have a worthwhile portfolio, your real estate investments must be treated the same as running any other business. Positive and measurable goals ensure accountability.

In my humble opinion, real estate is the single greatest vehicle for the average person to achieve financial freedom. That's why I am still actively investing in real estate and see this as my pension plan.

Key points to remember:

- ✓ A real estate investor is someone who buys real estate for investment purposes rather than for their primary residence.
- ✓ A real estate investor can be an active investor (doing hands-on work on their properties or hiring contractors) or a passive investor (hiring a property management company to handle the day-to-day work involved in maintaining their investment properties).
- ✓ Unlike owner-occupied home buyers, real estate investors are not emotional in their buying decisions. They also are more willing to write multiple offers.
- ✓ As an investor, you should set challenging yet realistic goals about how much property you intend to acquire.

Chapter 7

HOW TO FINANCE YOUR INVESTMENT PROPERTIES

When decide to become a real estate investor, one of your first steps will be figuring out how to pay for the property (or properties) you intend to purchase. Your decision to finance or pay cash will determine your return on investment, so finding the best financing option is critical.

As previously mentioned, if you are creditworthy, have a solid financial statement, and are employed, you have an amazing opportunity even in today's market to acquire a sizable portfolio. *Note:* If you are self-employed and don't have at least two years of tax returns, it may be a bit more challenging to obtain financing because your lender will want to look at recent tax returns to verify your income.

Can you invest in real estate if you have poor credit?

Although some real estate "gurus" have proclaimed that people can buy property even if they have no credit, poor credit, or no job, does that seem realistic to you? Would you sell a property you own that is in a family-friendly neighborhood to someone who has no credit? If a seller has a rundown property in an undesirable area and they can't sell it any other way, however, this may be their only option.

If you are using a real estate agent, can you imagine a seller being willing to sell a property without asking for a down payment and still paying a commission out of pocket? I have never met anyone who bought a property that was worth owning with no money down. Does it happen? It probably happens on rare occasions, but the claim that anyone can buy property with no money down is highly exaggerated.

In many instances, I have paid cash for a property or used a line of credit to purchase the property as well as cover fix-up costs. Once the work was completed, the bank appraised the property and I was able to refinance it for the exact amount of money I had invested. In effect, this was a "no money down" proposition that was available to me because I was creditworthy.

The key is that I bought an undervalued property and even after the fix-up cost the loan-to-value ratio was 60% of the appraised value—not a very risky proposition for the bank. This type of scenario is realistic if a buyer is creditworthy and has a solid financial statement to back it up. If not, it won't happen.

Have you established meaningful relationships with local banks or other financing sources? Ideally, you want to work with a lender or personal banker for in-house commercial loans who understands the real estate investment market and or is an investor. They may be very good at crunching numbers but have no clue of the big picture. If they lack this knowledge, you can either educate them or find a different personal banker or lender who meets your needs.

I have found that local institutions including community banks are much easier to deal with than nationwide banks, especially for lines of credit and commercial-type loans.

As you already know, investors prefer to use OPM (other people's money) as much as possible, so establishing good relationships with bankers will benefit you greatly.

Different options to purchase properties

1. *Cash* – Most of the investors I work with pay for their purchases with a line of credit that works the same as cash. They use the LOC to purchase property and make the necessary improvements, and then they get the property appraised and term it out with permanent financing. The most popular option is a commercial loan that is kept in house, amortized over 10 to 20 years with 5- to 7-year balloon. These types of loans are much easier to secure than other types of loans. Keep in mind that if you use a mortgage broker, they follow Fannie Mae or secondary market guidelines that limit the number of properties you can buy.

   The same process can be used when you buy a property with the intention of flipping it. Once the property is sold, you will use part of the proceeds to pay off the LOC and then move on to the next property and so on. When you do this, you don't need to get an appraisal.

   Let me give you an example that illustrates why refinancing is better than paying cash. If you buy a $100,000 property with cash and have no intention of refinancing you will lose the biggest benefits of all, which are the interest deduction and the power of leverage. With that same $100,000 you could be controlling $500,000 worth of real estate (five $100.000 properties). (See the example following item 10 below.)

2. *Equity line of credit or bridge loan* – This is the most popular way to purchase properties other than an outright cash offer. For anyone who has equity in their personal residence

or other collateral and a solid financial statement, this type of financing is very easy to obtain. Investors who flip properties can use a line of credit to cover the purchase price, remodeling, and other expenses. Once the property sells, the investor pays off the LOC and moves on to the next project.

3. *Commercial loans* – These types of loans can be used for residential properties but more typically are used for large properties such as apartments, office buildings, and everything else above four units. Underwriting in the commercial market focuses more on the property than on the income of the borrower, but the lender will still want to ensure that the borrower is creditworthy. As an example, if you are interested in purchasing a $5,000,000 apartment building, the lender will want to make sure that the income it produces will support the mortgage payment if anything goes wrong, in addition to making sure that the buyer is very solid financially. This type of loan is not likely to be issued to a first-time investor.

4. *Conventional mortgage* – What else can I say about conventional financing that you don't already know? You may not be aware that some lenders require more than the usual 20% down. In fact, the required down payment can be as high as 30% to 35%. It is best to check with several lenders, as some may offer special down payment programs for investors.

5. *Family, friends, and other individuals* – This form of financing is unique because of the relationship between the lender and borrower. Family members may pool their financial resources to invest as a "family activity." As another example, a family member may have discretionary

funds such as $100,000 sitting in the bank earning very little interest but could do much better by loaning the money for a set period and receiving a 5% to 7% return.

6. *Partnership* – Partnerships come in all forms. I have two partners in my real estate business. All three of us are equal partners who share in profits and expenses. You might know someone who is willing to take an ownership position but may not want to have any direct involvement in the project. Partners receive tax benefits based on their percentage of their investment (cash flow, appreciation, depreciation, and so on) as well as profits when the property is sold.
7. *FHA loans* – FHA loans are accessible to buyers who may not have enough money for a down payment on a conventional mortgage because the minimum down payment on an FHA loan is 3.5%. An FHA loan can be used to purchase an investment property up to four units if the purchaser plans to live in one of the units.
8. *FHA 203k loans* – This type of loan can be used to purchase a property that needs rehabbing. The buyer can use the money to finance repairs and other improvements. The 203k loan is available to an investor who is planning to occupy at least one of the units.
9. *Seller financing* – In some instances, it may be advantageous for a seller to partially finance the property, especially if it is owned free and clear (because the seller will receive tax benefits from issuing the loan). Although I haven't seen much seller financing, this would be a great option for a short-term loan, perhaps amortized over 15 years with a 5-year

balloon. It is common for a seller who has a free and clear property to record the deed of trust. However, you need to make sure the property truly is owned free and clear. If there is a loan against the property, the note can be called by the lender immediately through a "Due on Sale" clause.

10. *Hard money lenders* – If traditional financing is not obtainable, hard money lenders may offer a temporary solution. Any private individual can be a hard money lender. This type of loan is based on property value. The term of the loan is usually three to six months, and the interest rate is very high: 10% to 20%. Hard money lenders charge high fees for loans. In addition to paying the high cost of these loans, a borrower who is unable to meet the deadline for repayment may face foreclosure or must pay additional fees to renew the loan.

If you intend to build wealth, you should never pay cash for a property

When you pay the full price of a property in cash, you are limiting your ability to build wealth. Here's an example that illustrates my point. Let's say you pay $100,000 for a property in cash with no intent to refinance. If the property goes up in value by $10,000 during the first year, what is the return on your investment? 10%. Another way to look at it would be to figure out the cash on cash return after year one. For this purpose, let's say the cash flow before taxes is $3,525. Your cash on cash return would be $3,525/$100,000 = 3.525%.

What would happen if you purchased the same $100,000 property with a $20,000 down payment? If the property value goes up by $10,000, what is your return on investment in the first year? 50%. For the same scenario as above, you would have a cash on cash return of $3,525/ $20,000 = 17.62%.

Can you now see the power of leverage?

Although most investors will continue to rely on options 1–4, the preferred option is still number 1. The other options may be helpful for those who are not able to finance their purchase in a traditional way. Investors also might want to consider using funds from a Roth IRA to finance real estate purchases (see Chapter 14 for a discussion of this topic).

When you have your finances in order, you will be well on your way to achieving success in this business. Your real estate agent will take you more seriously and be willing to take the time to help you accomplish your wealth building objectives.

Key points to remember:

- ✓ Using a line of credit for a down payment and then getting an appraisal and obtaining long-term financing is the most popular option for purchasing investment properties.
- ✓ Deciding whether to pay cash or to use other people's money is critically important because the type of financing will affect your return on investment.
- ✓ If you are looking to build wealth, you should never pay cash for a property without refinancing it.
- ✓ In addition to traditional loans, investors may qualify for FHA loans if the property is four units or less. However, it will be very difficult to compete with cash buyers in a tight market if you use this type of loan.
- ✓ Some investors may choose to form partnerships or borrow money from friends and family members.
- ✓ It is essential for investors to form good relationships with local bankers who understand real estate investing.

Chapter 8

THE F-A-B-F-S/R SYSTEM: FIND, ANALYZE, BUY, FIX, SELL/RENT

Whether your intent is to buy and hold or flip, the F-A-B-F-S/R system described in this chapter will help you make good decisions along the way. The biggest mistake you can make is not using a system and trying to fly by the seat of your pants.

Hundreds of books have been written about investing in real estate and I have read some of them; however, most of my knowledge comes from practical experience. Like many others, I made a lot of mistakes early in my venture. I learned by trial and error, buying the wrong properties in areas I shouldn't have, paying too much for properties, spending too much on remodeling, and so on. Fortunately, real estate is very forgiving, and I learned from my mistakes.

Get off the starting block

If you don't take the next step, nothing will be lost and nothing will be gained. If you get in the "game," however, the opposite will be true. You will open a new and exciting chapter in your life and possibly become becoming a millionaire investor can be a reality. Along the way, you will enjoy all the benefits that real estate offers, including tax deductions and additional income.

In this chapter I will take you step by step through the system I have used in my own real estate business and shared with my clients for many years. This system will give you a solid foundation for building wealth and avoiding costly mistakes.

If you choose the right real estate agent and follow my system, you can avoid the trial-and-error stage and produce measurable and worthwhile results that can be repeated over and over.

The System

According to Business Dictionary.com, a system is "a set of detailed methods, procedures, and routines created to carry out a specific activity, perform a duty, or solve a problem."

To use my system effectively, you will need to develop clear criteria for identifying the properties you will consider, the properties you will buy, and the properties you will walk away from.

The types of properties that will generally offer the best opportunity for immediate equity are foreclosures, REOs, estate sales, properties that have been neglected and need cosmetic improvements, properties that have been tagged by the city for violations, and possibly properties that have been listed for several months and are vacant. There are lots of other ways to purchase properties such as auctions, "for sale by owners," wholesalers, and more.

Keep in mind that location, location, location should always be considered when deciding whether to make an offer or not. Buying real estate in various locations is a lot like buying blue-chip versus penny stock. Your real estate agent should be aware of the emerging areas in your communities and be able to identify available properties that you are likely to be interested in.

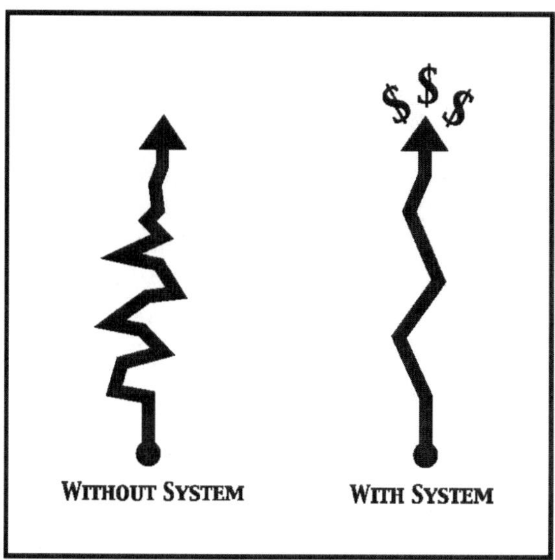

The goal is to purchase undervalued properties that have a big enough spread between the purchase price and potential value to let you achieve the desired profit.

Since investors come from all walks of life and have different reasons for investing, a one-size-fits-all strategy will not work. Factors to consider may include how much money you want to invest, your age, your needs, whether you are looking for short-term profit or long-term income, how much risk you are comfortable with, and so on. With the help of your real estate agent, you will need to develop your own set of criteria for choosing properties.

When all is said and done, if (1) you have the correct mindset; (2) your agent finds you deals; (3) your agent helps you analyze properties; (4) your agent helps you negotiate the deal; and (5) your desired properties get to the closing table, then you will be likely to get excellent results. If you choose the right agent early in the process, you will see how powerful the relationship between you and your agent can be for many years to come. It is a WIN-WIN: they help you accomplish your objectives and you help them make a good living.

My five-step system, F-A-B-F-S/R, is summarized briefly below. Each step will be described in detail in this chapter.

Step 1. **FIND** – Select a property that has investment potential. If the property is truly a great deal, you must act quickly or it will be gone. Keep in mind that you are competing with other investors for limited properties that are available. Does the property initially meet your objective of maximizing the profit given the risks? If the answer is yes, move to the next step.

Step 2. **ANALYZE** – Depending on the type of property, this step may be very easy to accomplish. If it is a single-family dwelling, comparable properties are the best indicator of the value after fix-up costs. If it's a multi-unit, more information is required to run the numbers. If the property passes the analysis, move on to writing an offer.

Step 3. **BUY** – Write the offer while paying attention to the bottom line. If your offer is accepted, follow through with the purchase and go to the next step.

Step 4. **FIX** – Make repairs and/or updates to get optimum rents or profits. Staying on budget is key.

Step 5. **SELL / RENT** – Flip quickly or rent the property after repairs have been made within the desired time frame and budget.

In the rest of this chapter, we will take a closer look at each of the five steps.

Step 1: Find a property

A key factor in finding an investment property is to base the decision on numbers, not emotion. Keep in mind that this is a business venture, not playtime. As an investor, you should buy a property because it is a good deal, based solely on the numbers. Will the property meet your short- and long-term financial objectives? Simply put, that means looking at cash flow, tax benefits for a rental, and whether or not the property is a good deal. What about if you are buying it to flip? To evaluate a potential flipper, answer the following questions:

1. What can the property sell for, based on prices of comparable properties in the same neighborhood?

2. How much will it cost to make the needed repairs and updates?

3. How much profit, realistically, do you want to make?

If you pay too much for a property or spend considerably more than the budgeted amount for the rehab, the desired profit may not become a reality.

Your real estate agent should be able to recognize a good deal. If they know and understand the local housing market, their knowledge will bring tremendous value to you. Experienced real estate agents who are also investors bring a wealth of knowledge based on experience, research, and education.

Different ways to find a good deal

Although those who haven't been in the investment game may have missed out on some excellent buying opportunities, it doesn't mean there are no deals available. Deals can still be found even though they are not as readily available as they were a few years ago. Investors who utilize a real estate agent should expect the real estate agent to spot the good deals that exist.

Multiple Listing Service (MLS)

There are many ways to find properties for investment purposes, but my primary choice is the MLS. Although the competition is quite fierce for properties with investment potential, on any given day your agent should be able to find properties that will meet your criteria. Sometimes searching the MLS four or five times a day instead of once a day will make a difference between finding properties or not.

Your agent may be able to find expired listings, properties that have been listed for 90 days and more, properties that have been reduced in price, properties that are vacant, not listed, and so on. They can search the Internet for terms such as *foreclosure, REO, cosmetics, estate motivated, must sell, as is, handyman, TLC, needs work, motivated,* and *cash only*. Keep in mind that what may be a good property for one investor may not be good for another. What criteria are important to you?

Your agent can network with other agents

If your real estate agent is a residential investment specialist, they are likely to network with other real estate agents who work with investors (not just agents in their own company). If they are engaged in this niche market, they know other agents who do the same thing. This is not about competition but about helping sellers sell their property in the shortest amount of time.

How many real estate agents in your own community specialize in investments? There are probably very few compared with the masses of real estate agents who compete fiercely for residential listings and sales. Get to know agents who list foreclosures and short sales.

Here are some of the ways your agent can be helpful to you:

1. *Word of mouth*

   They can let other agents know that they have buyers who are always looking for properties in need of repairs (cosmetic or major work). These properties make great flipping candidates or rentals. Perhaps these agents have no interest in working with investors. This can be a very effective strategy because other agents might not have a potential buyer for this type of property.

2. *Advertise*

   Some real estate agents may advertise in your local newspaper's real estate section that they have buyers who are looking for properties in any condition. They can also get a one-party listing.

3. *Visit the county assessor's website*

   Your agents can go to the county assessor and get a list of all the multi-units. This is a good way to identify people who own multiple properties or perhaps live out of state. These owners may be ready to sell properties that you are interested in purchasing.

Auctions

An innovative way to buy real estate is through online auctions. One of the main drawbacks of using auctions, however, is that they may prohibit you from going into the property. Inspections and due diligence are important aspects to consider. If you can't verify the condition of the property and figure out what kind of work it needs, making the wrong purchase could end up costing you dearly and becoming a disaster waiting to happen.

Even if you are able to find a property on your own, I highly recommend that you always try to utilize the assistance of a qualified real estate agent because they can help you reach your goals much faster.

Regardless of whether you are an experienced investor or just trying to get started, knowing where and how to find the right deals will be the biggest challenge you will face. This is especially true in a tight market where good deals are not as readily available.

There are several websites that you can search for properties in your community and in other states. Here are a few of the better-known websites that have property listings.

- *Craigslist.com* is a free website that has a Real Estate tab for property owners and real estate agents.
- *Auction.com* auctions all types of real estate, including foreclosures, REOs, short sales, notes, commercial real estate, luxury real estate, new construction, and land. These auctions take place online, locally on-site or in courthouses, as well as in live mega-auctions in meeting halls

- *Realtor.com* is the official site of the National Association of Realtors®. You can search through millions of listings compiled from over 800 MLS databases throughout the country. You are also given the option to search exclusively for foreclosures.

- *Zillow.com* is a very user-friendly website. To find property, you type in your search criteria. Your search can be as simple or as detailed as you wish. You can simply enter a location of the country for a basic search or you can type in factors such as type of property, price, and foreclosure status to do a more specific search.

- *RealtyTrac.com* focuses on foreclosures. You can search the latest foreclosure listings across the country as well as learn the basics of foreclosures. This site has ample information on everything from how to buy foreclosures to the latest news and statistics on foreclosures.

- *PropertyShark.com* provides property records. Property records are very useful when evaluating investment property because they contain important information such as the owner's name and address, the assessed taxes, square footage, and the purchase price.

- *Costar.com* is the number one provider of commercial real estate information. Visit this site to connect with the world's leading commercial real estate professionals.

- *Loop Net* is the most heavily trafficked commercial real estate marketplace online, with more than 8 million registered members and 5 million unique monthly visitors.

Note: Some of these sites are free and others require a subscription.

Why should you focus on finding good deals?

There is no reason for you to pay retail price for a property in the hope of appreciation. Purchasing an undervalued property makes more sense because it gives you instant equity or appreciation. Keep in mind that if the property is ready to go and needs very little improvement, an owner-occupied buyer will likely pay more for it than you would.

Whenever possible you want to buy properties where the value can be increased by doing some type of improvement. Suggestions are provided later in this chapter.

Your real estate agent should understand why it is so important for you to purchase properties that are good deals. There is no reason for you to chase properties that do not meet your criteria. There will be a property tomorrow that will be better suited.

I study the MLS on a regular basis and look at the properties that sold, and I am amazed to see how much money people paid for some of the properties. Always keep in mind that you make your money when you buy. Fall in love with the deal and not the property and you will never go wrong.

Do you know anyone who paid too much for a property? No amount of wishing or praying is going to make that investment worthwhile or profitable. Did they fall in love with the property or the deal?

What about someone who bought with the idea of yearly appreciation and then the market took a downturn and values decreased as in 2008? They will owe more than the property is worth. An investor should buy a property based on how much it is worth right away (after fix-up has taken place), and not what they hope it might be worth in the future.

Investors have different needs, objectives, and criteria. For example, some care mostly about cash flow while others are interested in the tax benefits. In my opinion, every investor should think about wealth building and retirement income. Always keep in mind that the reason you want to do this is for wealth building. Of course cash flow is important, but how much cash flow is necessary for you? Is $50 to $100 less cash flow a reason not to buy? If it is that important, perhaps you should not be investing at all. What is most important will whether the rent covers the mortgage.

Your defined criteria will keep you focused on buying only properties that meet your objectives. If you determine that a property meets your needs, don't get stuck in "analysis paralysis." Pull the trigger and have your agent write an offer.

Properties in family-friendly neighborhoods will always be in demand, and the opposite is true for properties located in high-crime or otherwise undesirable areas. Who will be the likely tenant of the property under consideration? Will it accomplish your long-term objectives? There are lots of things to consider.

Don't just ask your agent to find a deal for you; be more specific. What locations are you interested in? What about the number of bedrooms and baths, garages, price range? Do you want properties that are ready to go or only properties that need work? Make sure you give your agent enough specifics to guide their search.

Criteria may include any or all of the following: price range, location, schools, amenities/features, property condition, construction (brick or frame), number of bedrooms and bathrooms, with or without garages, close to a college or medical school, style of home or property, a property that needs minimal work and is virtually ready to rent, a property that needs updating to flip, and so on. But ultimately the property can be considered a good deal if it makes sense financially.

You now have enough information to establish a plan of attack. It's like digging for gold to find the types of properties you are likely to purchase.

Spotting an Attractive Potential Rental or Fixer-Upper

Look for these signs that a residential property is likely to be a good investment:

- ☐ Located in a desirable area
- ☐ The ugly duckling of the neighborhood
- ☐ Vacant and may be tagged by the city
- ☐ Good bones but needs updating
- ☐ Absentee owner
- ☐ Available through an estate or distressed sale or foreclosure
- ☐ Desirable floor plan with character and charm
- ☐ May have hardwood floors under the carpet
- ☐ Spacious kitchen that may need updating
- ☐ Three bedrooms, including a good-sized master bedroom

- Finished basement with enough room to add another bedroom by putting up a wall and adding an egress window

Bottom line: If minor improvements will increase the property value, the decision to buy is a no-brainer.

Classifying properties as A, B, C, D

As you evaluate properties it is important to use a consistent system. For our purposes we will classify properties as A, B, C, or D.

These letter grades are assigned to properties and areas based on characteristics such as age, property condition, growing or declining areas, appreciation potential, amenities, and potential rental rates, to name a few characteristics.

It's important for you to understand various property classes and areas and why a similar property in area D costs much less than one in area B.

It is important to recognize the values of similar properties in different areas and understand how these differences can affect your investment goals.

Characteristics of properties

Although assigning letter grades to properties can sometimes be more of an art than a science, the property classes will typically be characterized by the following characteristics:

"A" properties: These types of properties are like blue-chip stock. They tend to be newer properties built within the last five to fifteen years with the most up-to-date amenities and will typically demand the highest rents. There is no deferred maintenance. Older properties in excellent condition that are in extremely desirable areas also can fall into this category, as can properties located near universities, hospitals, major businesses, and so on.

"B" properties: These types of properties may be a notch or two below an A property. They may not have all the amenities. They tend to be a bit older and may not command as much rent. They may have some deferred maintenance. They usually have appreciation potential. A savvy investor can quickly raise the property's value by making minor improvements.

"C" properties: These types of properties are typically older properties built 30+ years ago with far fewer amenities. They may be a notch or two below a B. They may be in up-and-coming neighborhoods. Rents may be lower than for B properties. They usually have more deferred maintenance. The savvy investor can very quickly transform a C into a B by making minor improvements.

"D" properties: These types of properties are in undesirable areas such as high-crime neighborhoods. The neighborhood is a bigger problem than the condition of the property because properties can be improved but little can be done about the neighborhood.

D properties may have a lot of deferred maintenance. Rents are lower, and the quality of the tenants may not be great. Unless the neighborhood turns around, there will probably be little to no appreciation. They require intense management. These types of properties are not recommended for brand-new investors.

A lot of money is being made in this space, and although D properties are cash flow machines, they require a lot of attention and repairs. These properties can be compared to penny stock: high-risk, high-reward. An important consideration before buying this type of property is what kind of image you want to maintain in your community.

Characteristics of neighborhoods

Your real estate agent should be knowledgeable about areas that are improving as well as areas that are declining. Depending on the neighborhood, what may be a D property today could become a B property in a few years or vice versa.

When you evaluate areas, you can use a similar A, B, C, D classification system:

A – Newer growth areas

B – Older, stable areas

C – Older, declining, or stable areas

D – Older, declining, or potentially rapidly declining areas

These guidelines will help determine the property types and locations you are interested in. The key is to identify properties that will accomplish your investment goals.

In choosing a property, you should focus on properties in areas that are equal to or better than the class of the property itself (for example, a B property in a B or A area) and avoid properties in areas that are lower than the property class (for example, an A property in a C area). The area will have a great deal of influence on the stability of your portfolio over time and will determine whether it appreciates or declines in value during times of economic fluctuation. An A property is going to have a much harder time performing like an A property if it is in a C area, but a C property might perform better over time if it is in an A area.

If you are looking for investments with the highest appreciation potential and the best initial cash flow, you may consider looking for A and B properties located in A and B areas or in the path of progress. You will want to avoid properties in C areas. If you are not as interested in appreciation but are looking for investments with strong cash flow, then B and C properties in B and C areas would be the best fit.

If you are looking for a lot of cash flow and don't care about anything else, a D property may be an excellent option. Keep in mind these are only guidelines and your strategy should be based on your desired objectives.

Now that you're more familiar with the ABCs of property and location classifications and how they can affect the value of an investment, you will be able to more effectively select properties that can meet and exceed your investment goals. In summary, you need to decide what kind of image you want to maintain in your community. Do you want to be known as a slumlord or as someone who owns desirable properties that attract tenants who take pride in renting from you? Another way to put it is simply this: Would you point out your rental property to one of your friends?

Step 2: Analyze a property

The most important criterion for choosing a property is the financial component, and every offer made should be based on careful analysis to maximize profits given the risks.

Depending on the type of property that is being evaluated, the analysis can be very easy to do. If it is a single-family dwelling, the selling prices of comparable properties are the best indicator of value after fix-up costs. Multi-unit properties are evaluated differently.

A house is very simple to analyze. How much rent can you expect compared to the PITI (Principle, Interest, Taxes, and Insurance)? If a three-bedroom property rents for $900 and the PITI is $600, the cash flow is $300 a month before expenses. Is this a worthwhile investment or not? The simple answer is yes. You also should consider the financial impact of repairs, vacancies, and possibly property management. Bottom line: If the rent covers the expenses and there's money left over, wealth building is the outcome.

What if you are interested in buying a duplex or a fourplex? How would you determine whether it's a good deal? Running the numbers will tell you whether the subject property is a poor or good investment opportunity. More details on this topic can be found in Chapter 9.

To recognize whether a property is likely to be a good investment, consider cash flow, leverage, equity, appreciation, and risk.

1. Cash Flow

- Will this property produce the desired cash flow?
- What is the current rental market like?
- What is the vacancy history for this property?

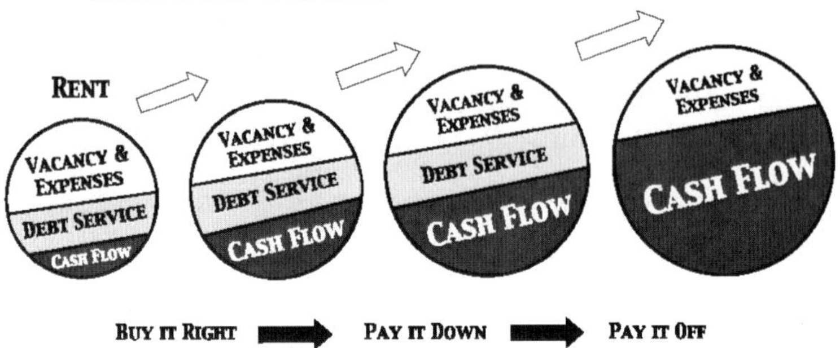

- How much is the down payment (10%, 20%, 30%, or more)?
- What is the interest rate on the loan?
- Will this property provide the desired income?
- How important is income now to as opposed to building wealth and generating retirement income in 10 to 20 years?
- Do you have another source of income?
- Is future equity more important?
- How will this property's cash flow compare with that of other potential properties?

You should take all of these factors into consideration when you are evaluating a property. For example, if you are analyzing several properties in the same neighborhood, ask yourself whether a $50,000 house that rents for $750 a month would be a better deal than a $100,000 duplex that rents for $1,050 per month or a $150,000 fourplex that brings in $2,000 per month. Instead of buying a duplex for $100,000, would it make more sense to purchase two $50,000 houses that will produce a combined rental income of $1,500 per month? Would the two houses cost more to maintain than the duplex would cost? If so, how much more? Which of these potential purchases would be a better investment for you?

There are no right answers to these questions, and you should decide what is most important to you. The property should accomplish your long-term objectives of wealth building, retirement income, and financial freedom, but cash flow should also be considered when you are looking at a potential purchase. Keep in mind that the above prices are for illustration purposes only and you can determine the appropriate values for your community and decide what is best for you.

2. Leverage

The less cash you must use as a down payment on each property, the more buying power you will have and the greater the opportunity to expand your portfolio.

Example of leverage:

- Investor A purchases a property for $200,000 cash. The property appreciates 5% in the first year ($10,000), so the return on the investment is 5%.

- Investor B purchases a property for $200,000 with a $20,000 down payment and a mortgage of $180,000. The property appreciates 5% in the first year ($10,000). Based on the initial $20,000 investment, the return on the investment is 50%. Investor B benefits greatly from the power of leverage.

3. Equity

Is the property offered at a huge discount? Investors should only buy home runs because a great deal will have instant equity.

Equity can take several forms, depending on the situation. All of the following types of properties could be great deals:

- A property that is undervalued
- A potential fixer-upper
- A rezoning opportunity
- A poorly managed property
- A foreclosure
- A short sale (a home where the purchase price is less than the amount owed by the seller)

There are many ways to create equity, but the easiest way is to buy a property that is a great deal.

4. Appreciation

If a property is a great deal, appreciation and equity will happen instantly. Buying in the right neighborhoods should minimize the risk if a good decision is made. In today's market, an investor should be able to purchase a property at 20% to 30% below or above the price that the same property sold for just a few years ago. Keep in mind again that you should not fall in love with the property but rather the deal.

5. Risk

To evaluate the amount of risk involved in buying a property, answer these questions:

- How much risk are you willing to take?
- What happens if your assumptions are not correct?
- Can you continue making the mortgage payment if you have a vacancy?

If you have done your due diligence and are comfortable with the level of risk involved in a potential purchase, you are well on your way to success as a real estate investor.

How to gather property information

Before you make an offer, it is important to know what factors contribute to the value of a property.

Accurate information is critical. The minimum information that would contribute to making an informed decision to either buy or pass on a property may include property details, financing, income generation, and expenses.

Property details. How old is the house or building (new, old, or run-down)? How many units does it have? Does the owner pay for the utilities or are the units separately metered? How much does the property cost? What are the expected costs for any repairs or updates?

Financing details. What is the loan amount, down payment, closing cost, loan terms (10, 20, 25, 30 years), and interest rate?

Potential income. How much income does the property generate (rent, laundry, vending machines, and so on)?

Expenses. What is the annual cost to operate the property? Include such things as taxes, insurance, maintenance, lawn care, snow removal, advertising, supplies, and so on. Also, consider setting aside funds to cover the cost of addressing issues related to deferred maintenance. A good property inspector can point out major repairs or expenses that the property is likely to incur in the future (for example, replacing the roof, furnace, central air units, and so on).

The income minus expenses determines the net operating income (NOI). NOI is one of the most important measures because it is used to determine a property's income stream. Concepts such as NOI, Cap Rate, debt coverage ratio, and others will be explained in detail in Chapter 9.

All the information you are working with must be accurate in order to determine whether a property is a great deal, an okay deal, or a horrible deal. The value of the property is directly related to how much income or profit the property produces for the investor.

It is not uncommon for a seller to provide numbers that are inaccurate. For example, they may inflate how much rent the property produces, not include any vacancies, and overlook certain maintenance expenses. In other words, by overestimating income and underestimating expenses, they make the property seem to be more valuable than it actually is.

Your agent will be critically important here and will help make a good decision or leave things up to chance. Make sure you have the best available information, all or most of which can be verified. (You may ask for a schedule E or tax returns for the past two years, for example.)

If the seller uses a property management company, they would be an excellent source of information and should be able to give you accurate information.

Are you familiar with the difference between *pro forma* information and actual information?

Pro forma means "estimated," and that is the information that is generally found on the MLS listing. You can analyze a property using pro forma, but it is better to base your analysis on actual information. Ideally, the pro forma will match the actual information.

Another piece of information to consider is the assessed value of the property. Are the taxes going up or down? It makes a difference on the bottom line if the income goes up and the expenses go down or vice versa.

It may not be a good idea to spend a lot of time analyzing a property before it is under contract. Depending on your experience as an investor and the complexity of the property, a detailed analysis can also be done during the next stage of the process.

Step 3: Buy the right property, based on your needs and objectives

Everything from the purchase agreement to closing happens during this stage. This is also your last chance for carrying out due diligence: for example, getting inspections by contractor(s) and so on to determine whether the expected remodeling costs are satisfactory to the buyer (of course, "satisfactory" will have a different meaning for each investor). I highly recommend having the sewer line inspected by a plumber using a camera. You might find out that the sewer line has shifted, is cracked, or is full of roots. If the sewer line needs to be replaced after you purchase the property, you could end up spending thousands of dollars.

Are you comfortable with the results of all the inspections? If the property passed the tests, will you be flipping or renting it?

What if the property is a multi-unit? The same due diligence may apply, but the decision to buy is also subject to insurance quotes or inspection of all units, as well as review and approval of leases, tax returns, rent rolls, and so on. The greater the amount of due diligence that can be accomplished during the analysis stage (step 2), the better. However, sellers are sometimes reluctant to provide the information until the property is under contract.

If the property meets the buyer's criteria, the offer is either written or not written at this stage. If the property will be used as a rental, the investor may be able to pay more than if it will be flipped.

For a rental, the bottom line is how much income the property will produce. Over the long term, paying $5,000 to $10,000 more for a property may not make much of a difference in the payment (PITI). An additional $5,000 at 5% interest with 20% down amortized over 20 years will be an additional $33 dollars a month in the payment. Sometimes buyers lose sight of the big picture and fail to realize that it might make sense to pay a little more for a property that will generate more income.

For a property that is being purchased to flip, a higher price makes a big difference and may not work. A price that is $5,000 to $10,000 higher than the investor's desired price may interfere with the ability to pay for a big chunk of the remodeling expenses. More information on flipping will be covered in Chapter 10.

How will the offer be written?

Will the offer be written as cash or conventional financing? Keep in mind that the preferred method of acquiring these types of properties is cash. This does not mean that an offer subject to a loan cannot compete with one from a cash buyer, but there is a good chance that even if the cash offer is lower it will get the nod. Sellers prefer cash offers because there is no need for appraisals to meet underwriting guidelines.

Other options for making cash offers include a line of credit or bridge loan if the subject property is not used as collateral. The collateral may be tied the buyer's personal residence, securities, or other assets. The buyer may be able to use this method to purchase and fix a property and then have it reappraised and perhaps pull all their money back in. The experience level of the investor, their creditworthiness, their financial statement, and so on will affect the feasibility of this approach.

A little-known fact is that investors can use their self-directed/Roth IRAs to purchase properties. A self-directed IRA requires account owners to make active investments on behalf of the plan. To open this type of account, an owner must hire a trustee or custodian to hold the IRA assets and be responsible for administering the account and filing required documents with the IRS. You will find more details on this topic in Chapter 14.

Lately, many real estate agents and investors have been getting frustrated because they can't find "deals." The common complaint is that when a property that is priced right hits the market, there are multiple offers that lead to a bidding war and the resulting price is drastically higher. This is totally different from the real estate market a few years ago when investors enjoyed the best opportunities in more than 40 years.

I am not saying that good deals are not available. It is all relative. You may pay more for a property, but rents are going up and so are the selling prices of flipped properties. The bottom line is that "lowball" offers are more likely than ever before to be a waste of time and to get rejected.

After the investor has purchased the property, the next step is to improve it.

Step 4: Fix the property

At this stage, the investor makes repairs and/or updates to get optimal rents or profits. Staying on budget during the remodeling process is crucial.

How does one know whether to make certain repairs? To illustrate how to make this decision, let's use an example of a $60,000 property that requires $15,000 in repairs for a total investment of $75,000.

Scenario 1

Let's say that comparable properties in the same neighborhood sell in the $110,000 range and the investor bought the property with the intention of flipping it. Carrying costs and selling expenses are $12,000 for a total expense of $87,000. The spread is a potential profit of $23,000 less tax consequences. Not a bad return in just a few short months. The credit line is paid back, and the investor moves on to the next deal.

Scenario 2

If the property is going to be used as a rental, it must be nice enough to attract tenants who will meet the investor's criteria.

Rental properties are intended to be workhorses and not race horses. In that regard, they should be upgraded to a level that sets the tone for how the tenant should treat the property. First impressions are important, and tenants should be just as picky about the property as the investor should be about the tenant. I believe that when tenants know what is expected, they will meet those expectations.

The more time that you spend upfront fixing up the property, the more pride the tenant will feel. When tenants see the owner taking an interest in the property, they will be more inclined to take good care of it. A property that is in disrepair sends a strong message that the landlord only cares about collecting the rent.

If a property is in poor condition, the tenants are not likely to be "blue ribbon." On the opposite side, well-maintained properties attract tenants that are likely to do their part to maintain the property.

Along these lines, every 2 to 3 months you should take the time to inspect your "investment" after giving the tenant at least 24 hours' notice. Inspecting the property will give you a lot of clues about how well your tenants are taking care of your investment. Your rental property represents a lot more than just cash flow. It is your wealth and retirement. Driving by the property is also a good idea.

Cosmetic versus structural problems

It may seem like an easy task to determine whether an issue with a property is a minor or major problem, but it depends on the viewpoint of the person who is doing the evaluating.

From a seller's perspective, all the issues with their property are minor problems. For many real estate agents, many problems are minor because they are common to a specific type of property of a given age and price range.

From a buyer's perspective, some problems are major, some are minor, and many are in between the two. As you are aware, you should look to home inspectors to provide you with input as to what are minor or major problems. Some investors may not use a home inspector but prefer to use a contractor instead.

Opportunities to purchase properties with minor or major issues can be found quite readily on the MLS. For the savvy investor, dollar signs are written all over them.

I've had clients who were able to purchase properties for pennies on the dollar because they required some foundation work, while other clients didn't want to touch these properties. Everything depends on the investor's mindset. Are they a first-time investor or someone who has flipped numerous properties and owns several income-producing properties? There can be opportunities galore for an investor who is receptive.

The lists that follow should make it easier to distinguish between cosmetic issues and major problems.

Cosmetic issues

- Paint interior/exterior
- Replace carpet
- Refinish wood floors
- Replace light fixtures
- Replace damaged kitchen cabinets
- Replace ceramic/vinyl floor
- Remove junk and debris from a property sold "as is"
- Landscape an overgrown lawn
- Fix property tagged by code inspector (the violation may be major or minor)
- Repair or replace siding
- Replace old appliances
- Update old bathrooms/kitchen
- Upgrade outdated electrical service

- Repair broken windows
- Do any other "quick-fix" repairs

If you take care of these simple improvements, you can expect your property values to increase dramatically.

Structural /major issues

For a beginner, any of the following issues with a property may be a deal breaker, but for the savvy investor they may signal a great opportunity. Regardless, one should proceed with caution.

- Problems with foundation or walls
- Plumbing issues including galvanized pipe, collapsed or cracked sewer line
- Leaning chimney
- Floors that slope
- Asbestos siding
- Rotting wood in the frame
- Lead paint
- Roof replacement: A roof may be serviceable but have two or three layers. If so, what will be the cost to replace the shingles?
- Buried underground oil tanks
- Old furnace and central air (HVAC) problems
- Mold
- Major termite damage

I'm sure you can think of other examples of major issues, but you get the point. The key is to understand that for some investors a minor cosmetic issue may be a problem, while to others a major structural issue may not be a deal-breaker. If you are a contractor and understand construction, you might not walk away from structural issues and may choose to buy a property that no one else wants. In some cases, a property with structural problems might as well have dollar signs all over it.

Here are a few easy and inexpensive ways to improve a property:

- Clean the house thoroughly, including the appliances.
- Paint the interior a nice neutral color.
- Replace linoleum with ceramic tile and replace old carpet (you can only clean it so many times).
- Replace kitchen cabinet knobs if necessary, as well as faucets that are old.
- Rake the yard, trim bushes, cut the grass, and plant some flowers to ensure that the property is presentable and has nice curb appeal.

Although there will always be opportunities to purchase properties that are good deals, it would be unrealistic for investors to expect to compete successfully with home buyers for properties that require little or no repairs. Buyers of owner-occupied properties will pay more than investors, perhaps even making offers above the seller's asking price.

In my experience, owner-occupied buyers are likely to walk away from properties that need work and are considered to have structural or major defects. These types of properties offer the best opportunity for good to great deals for real estate investors.

Some of my clients who are investors have walked away from certain properties that involved major remodeling tasks or structural issues, but there are investors for every type of property. Some may consider a new roof, furnace, bathroom, or foundation repairs to be a major project while others will think nothing of it.

If you are a new or inexperienced investor with no real construction knowledge, it might be best to avoid making an offer on a property that has major issues. Take time to find one that is more suitable for your needs. Properties are available for investors at all experience levels, and one that is better suited for you will show up.

Some people believe that real estate agents only care about their commission check, but I can assure you that agents who work with investors understand you are making a major financial decision. An agent who wants to continue working with you over the long term will provide advice that is in your best interests even if it means missing out on a sale.

Step 5: Sell/Rent

Obviously by the time you get to this step you have decided whether you want to rent the property or sell it. Your answers to the following questions will provide clues about the kind of landlord you will be:

1. Would you let one of your relatives live in the property in its current condition?

2. Would you be proud to show the property to one of your best friends? If the answer is yes, you are a proud property owner. Good for you.

Here are some good online and offline places where you can advertise a rental property

Renting a property quickly is key. The longer it takes to get the property rented, the lower the income for the investor.

- **Craigslist.com** is a site where people search for almost everything, including properties for rent or for sale. On the positive side, there is no charge and you can write your own ads and upload photos. On the negative side, you will get many inquiries and scammers.
- **Zillow.com** is the leading real estate and *rental* marketplace dedicated to empowering consumers with data, inspiration, and knowledge. You can post a rental through *Zillow Rental* Manager, which combines Postlets' free and easy-to-use features.
- **Hotpads** is a leading map-based apartment and home rental search brand, and it is a top destination for renters in urban areas across the United States
- **RentalHouses.com** is an online source of information about houses available for rent.
- **Airbnb.com** is a home rental site that connects a community of homeowners directly to customers seeking short-term rentals. Airbnb is a dominant player in the home rental sharing economy or peer-to-peer (P2P) activity of providing or sharing access to goods and services.
- **Apartments.com** and **Apartmentfinder.com** (both sites are under the same ownership) are popular sites that provide a free tool for users interested in long-

term rentals of apartments and condos. It offers deals and can provide upfront savings for users if they end up renting through the site.

- **VRBO.com** (Vacation Rentals by Owner) is a top-ranked site that specializes in vacation rental homes, apartments, condos, B&Bs, cabins, beach houses, villas, and so on.

- **Nextdoor.com** has carved out a unique space on the Internet as a private social networking site for local neighborhoods, with 80% of neighborhoods across the U.S. relying on the information and services it provides its members. It's a popular site for Realtors to brand their services and for landlords to list rentals to a highly engaged and active local community.

- **Facebook.com** has over 500 million users who participate in Facebook groups. These discussion groups focus on a variety of topics. Rental groups can be found by a highly customizable location search function. It's a great way to get the word out to your Facebook contacts about a rental property.

- People with **Pets.com** appeals to the approximately 72% of renters who own pets. The site is essentially a national directory of pet-friendly homes, apartments, and hotels. For renters, this site is free to use. For property managers, there is a charge for advertising your pet-friendly property.

- In addition to Facebook groups, consider posting on Instagram and Twitter. Properties can also be listed on Facebook's marketplace.

- Your local newspaper is a place to list rental properties, probably in the weekend edition. This is not the most affordable option, as ads can $25 to $50 or more.

- Local bulletin boards can be found at colleges, grocery stores, religious institutions, laundromats, and other locations.

- Word-of-mouth is a good way to connect with prospective tenants. If you own more than one rental property, ask your current tenants if they have a relative, friend, or co-worker who is looking for a rental.

- Place a "For Rent" sign in the front yard. If the property is located on a well-traveled road, hundreds of cars will see the sign daily.

- Using a Realtor or property management company is the most expensive way to advertise your property, as it will cost you anywhere from half a month to a full month's commission.

Regardless of the advertising source you use, it is important to respond to inquiries on a timely basis because quality tenants will have many options available to them. If you don't call or email back promptly, another landlord will beat you to it.

Bottom line: In finding tenants, make sure to do your due diligence. If you take any shortcuts, you are likely to regret it later. Take your time with each applicant and make sure you follow the same procedures with every applicant so that you won't run into any discrimination problems. You should also become very familiar with your local state's landlord-tenant laws.

Be aware that some tenants will be less than honest about their backgrounds or past issues, so due diligence is critical. The fact that they drive a nice car or wear nice clothes is not a good reason to overlook everything. If they have cash for the first month's rent and security deposit, a red flag should go up. It is also important to verify the information they provide about their previous landlord. You can do this by going to your county assessor to see who the owner of record is. I have caught a few applicants listing a relative as the landlord in an attempt to conceal the fact that they had been evicted.

A word of advice: You don't have to be a friend to your tenant, but it is your responsibility to be friendly and respectful.

How should you screen prospective tenants?

Careful selection of tenants will greatly improve the chances of succeeding in this business. You need to figure out what type of tenant you want. I prefer tenants who are commensurate with the quality and condition of the property. It is a huge mistake to rent to anyone without doing the necessary due diligence. There are numerous tenant screening services available to help you determine whether someone is qualified to rent a property.

Credit checks, criminal checks, landlord verifications from two previous landlords, and employment verifications are all important.

Probably the least important screening tool is the credit check. Keep in mind that if everyone had good credit there would not be any reason to have a rental business. Your gut instincts can also tell you a lot about a potential tenant.

Renting to anyone without verifying information will increase the risk that your property will be trashed. A good tenant will leave the property in just about rentable condition. The opposite will occur with a poor tenant whom no other landlord would rent to.

Sampling of Tenant Screening Services

- **Zillow.com:** The Zillow Rental Manager application and screening tool simplifies the application process and includes background and credit screening.
- **Myrental.com:** An innovative suite of tenant screening services including renter eviction.
- **Applyconnect.com:** Online screening services and tenant credit checks to help you separate the good renters from the bad.
- **Experian.com:** Industry-leading provider of tenant verification and *tenant background check* solutions.
- **Zumper.com:** The easiest way to screen prospective tenants. *Services* including *landlord credit check,* eviction, and criminal checks.
- **Rentalhistoryreports.com/small-landlords/tenant-screening:** Try the leading small landlord tenant screening service. We've pretty much seen it all and know how to help you fill your properties with the best tenants.

- **Tenantsreports.com:** Our mission is to provide a *tenant screening* solution with the most accurate tenant reports, fastest results, supported by the *best* customer *service.*

- **Nationaltenantnetwork.com:** *Helps* property owners and managers make the best leasing decisions possible.

Note: The author does not promote one service over the others, and readers should decide which service will best serve their own needs.

Some questions to ask potential tenants even before you show the property

When potential tenants call to view your rental, you should have a set of preliminary questions to ask that will help you separate the good renters from the bad. You will save a lot of time by showing your property only to tenants who meet your criteria. It is important that you use the same questions with all tenants so that you are not accused of discrimination.

Question 1: Why are you moving?

This question can tell you a lot about the tenant. Listen for legitimate reasons for moving, such as a job change or wanting a bigger home. Look for red flags such as being evicted or complaining that their current landlord doesn't take care of their property.

Question 2: What is your move-in date?

This can tell you a lot about the tenant. If the tenant wants to move in tomorrow, they may not be the most responsible person as most landlords require 30 days' notice to terminate a lease. There may be special circumstances such as a job transfer, a pay cut, or domestic abuse, but in general, responsible tenants will start their search for a property at least 30 days before their anticipated move-in date.

Question 3: What is your monthly income?

This question can help you determine whether the prospective tenant will be able to afford the property. Most people spend between 30% and 35% of their overall gross income on rent and utilities, not including renter's insurance. Keep in mind that monthly income may not tell the whole story about the prospective tenant's financial resources. Having a large amount of debt could reduce their ability to pay on time. The credit report will show you who their creditors are.

Question 4: Will you have the security deposit to hold the property and first month's rent before you move in if approved?

This will tell you about their financial situation. A prospect that doesn't have a full deposit and first month's rent will probably have problems paying the rent in the future. You do not want to start a tenant relationship where the tenant already owes you money.

You should never allow a tenant to move in without paying the full deposit and rent. Do not negotiate or make exceptions to this rule. Always require the full amount before move-in.

Question 5: How many people will be living in the property?

If a family has 2 or 3 kids, a two-bedroom house will probably be too small. Keep in mind that more people will mean more wear and tear. If the property has a finished basement but does not have an egress window, make sure you stipulate that under no circumstances can anyone sleep in the basement. You don't want any potential legal issues.

Question 6: Do you have references I can contact, such as your current and former landlord?

If the prospective tenant hesitates or make excuses for not being able to provide references, they are probably hiding something. References from an employer or current pay stubs for the last two pay periods are also important.

References from their current landlord only may not tell you the whole truth because they may be trying to get rid of the tenant. It is also advisable to verify who the owner of the property is through your county assessor's website and see if the landlord they gave you is the owner of record. Sometimes a prospective tenant will put a relative as the landlord, and of course they will give a glowing report such as "I hate to lose them."

Question 7: Is there anything I need to know about you as I run the credit and background checks?

If they tell you upfront that they did something stupid as a young adult such as shoplifting or that they got caught doing drugs and spent time in jail, it will be your call to make. Everyone deserves a second chance, and if they haven't had any issues and have steady employment use your gut and decide. You must have the prospective tenant sign a form giving their permission to run these checks. Verbal consent is not binding.

Question 8: Have you ever been evicted?

While the prospective tenant may not tell the truth, this question is still worth asking. Directly asking the prospective tenant if they have been evicted will give them the opportunity to explain the situation. Good people can fall on hard times and the eviction may have happened several years ago. If it happened long before the two previous landlord verifications you may want to use your discretion. If the eviction was for causing damage or excessive noise, these behaviors probably have not changed.

Question 9: Do you have any pets?

If you have a "no pets" policy, the prospective tenant with a pet most likely is not going to get rid of their pet. If your policy allows pets, it is important to find out what kind of pet it is, and you will want to see it. If they own a Pit Bull or Rottweiler, check with your insurance company to see if your policy will cover you if the dog bites someone. If you allow pets, we recommend requiring renters insurance. Make sure the insurance policy covers damage or injury caused by pets and that you are also an assignee. As the owner of the property, you don't want to be liable for anything. Renters insurance typically covers liability for dog bites on the property.

If the pet is a cat, it may or may not be a problem. The current trend is to charge pet rent instead of a pet deposit. The pet rent can be $25 per month or more per pet. (A deposit is not considered income by the IRS, but pet rent is). Always follow up with an inspection, as they may move in without their pet but a couple of months later you may drive by the property and see their pet.

Question 10: Do you have any questions?

This will give the tenant a chance to ask questions about your property, your screening process, or anything else that comes to mind. This is important because even if the tenant answered all of your questions to your satisfaction, the tenant also must have enough information to feel comfortable living in your property.

In conclusion, the above questions should give you enough information to determine whether you want to show your property to a prospective tenant. If your time is limited and there are many applicants, you may want to schedule an open house for everyone who has met your criteria.

Is it important to require tenants to sign a lease?

A lease is the contract between a landlord and a tenant. The lease sets forth the rights and responsibilities of both the landlord and the tenant.

The lease allows the tenant to occupy and use the property for a specific period of time. In return, the tenant generally pays rent.

The lease may set forth other duties and responsibilities of the landlord and tenant. Once both parties have signed the lease, both are bound by its terms.

What should a lease include?

1. Names of the tenant, the landlord or the landlord's agent, and the person or company authorized to manage the property
2. Address of the property and what appliances, if any, are included
3. The amount of rent required, date when the monthly payment is due, any grace period, and any late charges or nonsufficient funds fees
4. How the rent should be paid (check, money order, or cash)
5. Methods for terminating the agreement prior to the expiration date and what, if any, charges will be imposed

6. The amount of the security deposit
7. Whether the tenant or landlord pays for utilities
8. Rules and regulations such as pet rules (pet deposit), pest control, and many others
9. Methods of resolving maintenance issues

A sample lease is provided in the Resources section near the end of this book.

Important: If your property has a basement, especially a finished basement or a separate room in the basement, it must have an egress window if it will be used as a bedroom. If there is no egress window, your lease must stipulate that sleeping or using the room as a bedroom is a violation of the lease. Keep in mind the potential for a lawsuit if there's no escape access in case of a fire, flood, or other emergency.

Key points to remember:

- ✓ Success in real estate investment is more likely when you follow a system.
- ✓ You can follow the same five steps in this system over and over: Find, Analyze, Buy, Fix, Sell/Rent.
- ✓ There are many ways to connect with prospective renters both online and offline.
- ✓ Thorough screening of new tenants will help you avoid property damage and nonpayment of rent.
- ✓ A lease is designed to protect both the property owner and tenant.

Chapter 9

DEFINING FINANCIAL TERMS: THE NUMBERS MATTER

To become successful in this business, you will need to become familiar with several financial measures or formulas that apply to investment property. Even if you are not a "numbers person," you will need to acquire this knowledge because you will be making some of the most important financial decisions you are likely to make in your lifetime. You will probably be investing more money in real estate than you do in the stock market.

If you don't know how to evaluate a property, how will you know whether it is likely to be a good investment? Remember that successful real estate investors make their decisions based on money, not emotion.

Taking time to run the numbers will make a difference. I'm sure there are far more investors who don't take the time to evaluate an investment than those who do, but to me that is the quickest route to disaster.

Why not take the time to evaluate an investment opportunity correctly? If you "wing it," a lot of money may go down the tubes.

The information in this chapter is essential for you to absorb. I realize that there are more complicated formulas that I don't even understand, but familiarizing yourself with the basic ones offered in this chapter (such as net operating income, capitalization rate, debt coverage ratio, cash on cash return, vacancy and credit loss, just to name a few) will go a long way.

Getting down to business

How can you figure out whether property A, B or C is likely to be the best investment? A series of calculations will have to be performed to determine if the investment is likely to be a good one. After you run the numbers, you will be able to say, "According to my analysis, this property is (or is not) likely to be a good investment."

Analyzing a single-family dwelling is very easy. What is the total cash flow after paying the taxes, insurance, mortgage, and so on? After making these payments, the amount that is left over from the rent payment is cash flow. How much cash flow on a monthly basis will be acceptable to you: $50, $100, $200, or $300? Probably $50 or $100 will not be enough, but $200 should work. What do you think? Remember your "Big Why": wealth building, retirement income, and financial freedom.

The most common way to determine the value of a single-family dwelling is for your agent to provide you with comparables. For example, if a property can be purchased for $100,000 while others in the same subdivision are selling for $150,000, it may be a very good deal. Let's say it will require $15,000 worth of repairs, bringing the total investment to $115,000. Still sounds like a good deal to me. What do you think? Would it be a good investment if you would get $35,000 equity just by buying the undervalued property? This would be an example of making your money when you buy. Remember Rule #1: Fall in love with the deal and not the property.

However, a multi-unit property (such as a duplex or apartment building) is valued differently from a single-family dwelling. Its value is directly related to the property's income and expenses.

Would it be possible for a multi-unit to increase in value in the same general area as the example above while houses are declining in value? Yes, because multi-units are valued by income and expenses, overall condition, and so on. A financial analysis is critically important to make the determination.

What if two identical multi-unit properties are for sale one block apart from each other? Property A has deferred maintenance and rents that are well below market, and Property B is in very good condition and rents that are close to market rents. You are considering writing an offer but want to determine how much you should offer, and which property would be a better investment. You are seriously thinking of writing offers on both. Can you see why running the numbers is important?

Commercial-type properties such as large apartment buildings, industrial properties, and strip shopping centers require much more information before the analysis can be done properly.

Steer clear of these pitfalls

Remember, successful investors fall in love with the deal rather than the property and avoid making costly mistakes. Some of the most common mistakes made are listed below. (You can probably think of others.)

Mistake # 1: Analysis paralysis

Many people never take the first step toward building wealth or making a living in real estate because they suffer from analysis paralysis. Regardless of whether you're in a seller's market or a buyer's market, a property that is a good deal will not stay on the market for long. It is important to get the property under contract before you put much time and effort into analyzing it. A good contingency would be "subject to inspection by contractor to determine remodeling costs satisfactory to buyer within ___ days upon acceptance of offer." The word "satisfactory" has different meanings for different investors.

Mistake #2: Fudging the fix-up cost

Some investors underestimate the fix-up cost and talk themselves into moving forward with a purchase while others overestimate it to justify backing away from the deal. Investors may also forget to include the carrying costs, insurance, interest, taxes, and so on. Make sure the estimated fix-up cost is realistic. Don't fudge the numbers to make the deal cash flow or the rehab pay off. Buying or not buying without good information or facts doesn't make sense. Take time to perform the appropriate due diligence.

Mistake #3: Overestimating the rent

Sometimes rents are overestimated. What is the current market rent for the area? Is the estimated rent above or below market rates? If it is under market, can the rent be increased? Is it better to buy a property with below-market rents or one with above-market rents? When a unit becomes vacant will it be easy to rent, or will the rent have to be reduced?

Mistake #4: Overestimating the property's value

Don't overestimate what the property is worth. Can the property be purchased at a drastic discount or perhaps for a few thousand dollars less than the asking price? Plan for the unknown and be conservative in your estimate. If you know the area and the prices for similar properties it should be easy to determine whether the property is a good deal. If it is a multi-unit, different factors will come into play.

Mistake #5: Failing to recognize a great deal

A deal is a deal any way you look at it. Learn how to spot a great deal and then act on it. See mistake #1.

Mistake #6: Not paying attention to a property's location

Remember the adage about the three most important features of real estate: location, location, location. Is the property in the A, B, C, or D category (as described in Chapter 8)? Failing to consider where the property is located could be the costliest mistake of all. If an investor is selling the property and if it is such a good deal, why are they selling it? Perhaps they want to make a quick profit. Maybe they want to pass on the deal to another investor who can take the project to the next level. Maybe they just purchased it last week and are wholesaling it. I purchased several properties and made $10,000 in a few days without doing a thing to them.

Mistake #7: Underestimating the time required to fix up a property

Some investors underestimate how much time it will take to fix and flip a property, and therefore the project's objective may be in jeopardy. It is always better to plan for the unexpected.

Mistake #8: Letting fear hold you back

Nothing ventured, nothing gained. Arm yourself with knowledge and act quickly when you spot a great deal. Money and wealth are found on the other side of fear.

Mistake #9: Doing everything yourself

The biggest blunder of all is for the investor not to utilize the services of a knowledgeable real estate agent. I have listed properties that were purchased from "for sale by owners" that needed a lot of work. The buyers overpaid, and what they thought was going to be a profit-making proposition turned out to be the opposite. Ouch!

How to determine whether a property is a great deal

Your evaluation should consider the following aspects of a potential purchase: cash flow, leverage, equity, appreciation, and risk.

1. Cash flow

- What is the purchase price?
- What are the taxes?
- What is the estimated cash flow?
- What is the condition of the rental market in the vicinity of the property?
- What is the vacancy situation?
- What is the down payment?
- What is the interest rate?
- What is the net operating income (NOI)?
- Is the property a house, duplex, fourplex, or something else?

All of these factors should be considered in evaluating whether a property will provide income. How does the cash flow for this property compare with that of other potential investment properties? For example, does a $50,000 house that rents for $750 per month have a better income potential than a $100,000 duplex that rents for $525 per side for $1,050 total rent per month? How about a fourplex that costs $150,000 and brings $2,000 per month in the same neighborhood? Which of these properties is the best investment?

In addition to answering questions about the property itself, you need to answer the following questions about your own financial goals:

- How important is income to you?
- Do you have other income?
- Are you more interested in reducing your taxes than in earning income?
- Do you need more income now or in the future?

There are no right or wrong answers to these questions, but they are all factors that should be considered when looking at a potential purchase.

2. Leverage

The lower the down payment, the more properties one may be able to purchase. Banks may no longer be open to financing 100% of the property value, but it is not uncommon for them to require a loan-to-value ratio of 70% to 85%. Keep in mind that the more solid your financial statement and assets are, the greater the likelihood that the bank will structure the loan with more favorable terms.

3. Equity

There are many ways to create equity, but the easiest one is to buy a property that is a great deal.

4. Appreciation

Buying in the right neighborhood will increase the likelihood of a successful investment. In today's market, it is not uncommon to buy a property for 20% less than the price at which a comparable property would have sold just a few years ago. Under normal conditions, the average rate of appreciation is 2% to 4% yearly, and it would take five to ten years for a property to appreciate 20%. There's no need to wait for a property to appreciate because you should be able to find deals every day.

5. Risk

What happens if your assumptions are not correct? Will you be able to continue making the mortgage payment if there's a vacancy, for example?

What information is needed to analyze a property?

The first step is to understand the factors that contribute to property value. Gathering accurate information can help you determine whether a property is likely to be a good investment, but ultimately you must decide whether a property is the right investment for you.

1. Property details

This information includes how old the property is, number of units, square feet, whether the utilities are separate or on a single meter, whether the property includes garages that can produce additional income, whether it has laundry facilities (coin-operated), and so on.

2. Purchase information

What is the asking price, how much rehab work is needed, and how much deferred maintenance does the property have? The better the condition of the property, the more rent you can expect.

3. Financial details

Will you be purchasing the property with cash or obtaining a loan? If a loan will be needed, what are the loan amount, down payment, interest rate, and closing costs?

4. Income

How much income does the property produce from rent payments and from the laundry, garages, and so on?

5. Expenses

What are the costs to operate the property, such as maintenance, property taxes, insurance, property management, and so on?

Difference between pro forma and actual value

The value of a property is closely tied to how much income it produces. Knowing this, some sellers will provide financial information that is inaccurate. For example, they may overestimate rental income and neglect to mention that the maintenance expenses are much higher than the estimate. This scenario makes the property seem more valuable than it really is.

One of the most important measures for determining property value is the NOI or net operating income, a topic that will be discussed later in this chapter.

The more information you have gathered, the better your chances of making a good decision. How can you ensure that you have the information needed? Actual data is critical for making a good analysis, but there are some things that can easily change the picture. Initially, you may be able to use the pro forma data, but the estimated numbers will need to be verified by actual numbers.

One common way to verify information is to ask the seller to provide tax returns and maintenance records. Don't be surprised if the seller refuses (in which case a red flag should go up). If they do provide the information, it should be like the pro forma.

What happens if the property's assessed value goes up or down? Lower taxes mean higher income and higher taxes mean lower income. Small changes to income and expenses can make the difference between a poor, okay, or great investment.

Where can you find the information you need?

Property details: The seller should be willing to provide whatever information is needed. The assessor's office has the property details.

Purchase information: The seller has the property listed for a certain price or you probably know what he or she is asking. The most important information is the assessment of deferred maintenance or updating needed for the property to meet or exceed your income requirement.

The better the property, the more updating it will have had, including big-ticket items such as a new roof, HVAC system, windows, appliances and so on. Such a property will have a higher purchase price than one that is the opposite. A property inspection is worthwhile even if you are an experienced investor, because you never know what kinds of hidden defects will be revealed.

Financial details: How will the property be purchased? A cash offer is easy to deal with, but if the offer is subject to a loan it is important to talk to the lender (ideally, a local bank) to determine down payment requirements, term of loan, interest rate, and closing costs, and to obtain a pre-approval letter or proof of funds.

Due diligence

It is imperative that the seller provide any information that may be requested so that you can analyze the property to determine its investment potential.

Don't rely exclusively on the pro forma. If the seller uses a property management company, accurate information should be readily available from that source. Keep in mind that the owner of the property management company should also be a licensed broker who will avoid playing games with information because it could cost them their real estate license.

In addition, a home inspector/contractor can identify any potential repairs or big-ticket items that will need to be replaced in the future.

If you are using a real estate agent, they can gather the information that will be necessary to analyze a property to determine whether it is a good deal. The listing agent should have access to the information.

For a residential listing, a CMA (comparative market analysis) is easy to do. Determining the value of a multi-unit is more complicated because it reflects the income that the property produces as well as the expenses involved in operating the property.

When I go on a listing appointment, my job is to gather the information needed to determine a range for a listing price. First and foremost, I need information on the property's income and expenses. In addition, I ask the seller what he or she thinks the property is worth. If my analysis determines that the property is not worth as much as the seller thinks it is, the listing price will have to be adjusted downward. It is pointless to list a property that is unrealistically overpriced.

Determining property income

Net operating income (NOI) is the total income the property generates after expenses. NOI does not consider the debt service (principle and interest payment to the lender).

A property's income could come from several sources including rents, laundry machines, vending machines, and garage rental, or it could come only from rents.

Since most of a property's income will come from rents paid by the tenants, it is imperative that vacancies are taken into consideration.

Depending on where the property is located, its condition, and other factors, vacancies may be higher or lower than average. It is next to impossible for any property to operate at 100% efficiency (no vacancies at any time), and turnover will occur. Minimizing turnover is the key to maximizing income. Satisfied tenants tend to stay longer than dissatisfied ones.

The better the property is maintained and the more desirable its location, the lower its vacancy rate will be. Properties that have higher rates of tenant turnover are costlier to operate in terms of time and money.

If a property shows a much higher vacancy rate than similar properties in the same area or if the rents are lower than other properties, it is important to determine why this is so. Is the property in poor condition? What amenities does it offer? If similar properties have garages and new appliances while this one does not, this might explain why the rents are lower.

On the other hand, the rents may be lower because the seller is not very savvy. Perhaps he or she has owned the property for a long time, has long-term tenants, and simply has not raised rents for many years. There are many unknowns that require further investigation.

As part of your due diligence, make sure you are provided with the rent roll for the property, which is a list of tenants, lease expiration dates, and monthly rents. Also ask to see the leases, as they can tell you a lot.

If you are an experienced and savvy investor, there could be an opportunity to increase the value of the property simply by raising rents or by doing minimal updates that don't require spending thousands of dollars. Simple improvements such as new paint, countertops, ceramic tile in kitchen and baths, new carpet or refinishing the wood floors may make a difference.

Your due diligence should examine all the factors that will determine whether the property will meet your short- and long-term objectives.

Determining property expenses

The expenses for operating a rental property typically will break down into the following categories:

1. Property taxes (easy to determine)
2. Insurance (easy to determine through a quote from the agent)
3. Maintenance

Maintenance expenses may include lawn care, painting, gutter repairs, plumbing, roof repairs, HVAC, appliances, and any other repairs that are required to keep the property in good working order. A property's future expenses will be affected by its overall condition and the amount of deferred maintenance.

A nice property attracts good tenants, and a property with a lot of deferred maintenance does not. Although not spending money on maintenance makes the property's income look better in the short term, in the end it is costly. It is impossible for a property to have no maintenance expenses. If the maintenance information provided for a property is minimal, you should include a 10% maintenance factor as an expense, based on the Gross Scheduled Income.

As you assess the condition of each property, ask questions like these: How old is the roof? What about the HVAC system, appliances, and electrical system (fuses or circuit breakers)? When you preview the property you will see whether it has new or old windows. Are the kitchen and bathroom original or have they been updated? Is the plumbing galvanized or copper? If these big-ticket items have been updated, future maintenance expenses will be lower.

But keep in mind that when a property has not been well maintained, there may be dollar signs written all over it for the savvy investor. Such properties can sometimes be purchased at huge discounts, illustrating the truth of the saying, "You make your money when you buy."

4. Advertising

Likely this should not be a major expense, particularly if the property has a low vacancy rate. How much does it cost in your area to place an ad in the newspaper? There are also online sites that will allow you to advertise the property to prospective renters at little or no cost, as discussed in Chapter 8.

5. Supplies

This category of expenses involves anything needed to fix up a rental property to maintain its current value. Examples might include tools, drywall, plywood, paint and so on. The list could be endless.

6. Legal and professional fees

Most investors will utilize a tax professional to prepare their taxes and an attorney to assist in evicting a tenant or preparing legal documents such an LLC. These professional fees are tax-deductible business expenses.

7. Property management

Will you be managing the property yourself or using a property manager? You can check with local property managers to determine their fees. Some will charge 6% to 10% of rents, depending on the services they provide. Detailed information on property management is provided in Chapter 11.

8. Utilities

Who pays for the gas, water, and electricity in the units? In houses or duplexes, utility bills are generally paid by the tenant. If the property owner pays for the utilities, this is a difficult number to determine when budgeting from year to year. You can verify the cost of utilities by calling the utility companies, as it is public information. If the property is an apartment building it may have separate utilities for each unit (gas and electricity), but water will not be billed separately.

9. Among all the expenses involved in operating a rental property, two of the most powerful tax deductions are interest and depreciation.

Interest. Any interest paid during the year is deductible. Buyers who pay cash miss out on this huge benefit.

Depreciation. One of the largest tax benefits for an investor comes in the form of depreciation. The IRS allows investors to take a tax loss every year based on depreciation over the useful life of the asset, known as the cost recovery period. Depreciation can reduce an investor's taxable income by thousands of dollars each year.

The property itself can be depreciated at a steady rate for 27½ years for residential-type properties (four units or less) and 39 years for commercial properties.

Land that the property sits on is classified as a non-depreciable asset.

Personal property, which includes things such as appliances and carpets in rental units, can be depreciated over 5 years.

Land improvements such as shrubs, fences, sidewalks, driveways, and landscaping can be depreciated over 15 years.

Anyone contemplating the purchase of an investment property should seek the advice of a competent and knowledgeable attorney and tax advisor.

Sample property analysis and definition of terms

After tracking down the numbers, you can analyze a property for every important financial measure to determine whether it is likely to be an excellent, good, okay, or poor investment.

To make it easy for you, I have included a "Running the Numbers Analysis Form" in the Resources section near the end of this book. In the sample form, the only sections you will need to change are in the highlighted areas. Use the "Cost Recovery Depreciation" table in the Resources section to figure out the depreciation for Year 1.

When you are analyzing a property, the outcomes that you can predict with some degree of certainty are only for the first year after purchase. Anything after that is speculative.

Here we go!

Sample Property: Parker Duplex

Purchase price	$120,000
Down payment	$ 24,000
Term	20 years
Interest	6.5%
Closing costs	$ 3,600
Total investment	$ 27,600
Income from rents	$850 monthly rent per side = $20,400/yr.
Other income	None
Vacancy and credit loss	10% ($2,040)

Expenses	
Taxes	$ 2,997
Maintenance	$ 1,800
Insurance	$ 900
Repairs	$ 100
Lawn care / Snow removal	$ 200
Utilities	$ 100
Advertising	$ 50
Supplies	$ 200
Total expenses	$ (6,347)

Formulas for analyzing a rental property

1. Gross Scheduled Income: This is the total annual income that would be produced if all units were rented and rent was collected from every tenant. It represents the highest possible income collection for the property in its current condition.

Example: $20,400 income potential

2. Vacancy and Credit Loss: This is the income that will be lost due to vacant units (vacancy) or non-payment of rent (credit loss).

Example: $20,400 x 0.10 = $2,040

3. Gross Operating Income (GOI): This is the gross scheduled income, less vacancy and credit loss, plus income from other sources such as coin-operated laundry equipment, vending machines, and garage rentals.

Example: $20,400 – $2,040 = $18,360

4. Operating Expense (OE): This is the cost associated with operating the property, including such things as property taxes, maintenance, insurance, repairs, lawn care / snow removal, utilities, advertising, supplies, trash removal, property management, and so on. Operating expense does not include debt service, income taxes, or depreciation.

Example: $6,347

5. Net Operating Income (NOI): This is one of the most important measures because it represents the return on the purchase price of the property. Additionally, NOI can be used to as a strategy to increase value. For example, you can improve NOI by increasing the rent and decreasing the expenses whenever possible. To calculate NOI, you simply take the gross operating income and subtract the operating expenses.

Example: $18,360 – $6,347 = $12,013

***Note:* Do not include debt service or capital expenditures in NOI.**

Capital Expenditures: These are basically "one-time" costs that are not part of the day-to-day operations of the property. This category includes expenses such as installing new windows, replacing the roof, putting in a new driveway, and so on.

6. Cash Flow Before Taxes (CFBT): This figure is calculated by taking net operating income, subtracting debt service and capital expenditures, and adding loan proceeds (if any) and interest earned (if any). It represents the annual cash flow available before income tax deductions are considered. Cash flow is the money that the property generates or absorbs. Even if the tax return shows a loss, the actual cash flow of the property may show profits, or vice versa.

Formula:

Net Operating Income – Debt Service – Capital Expenditures

+ Loan Proceeds (for loans to finance operations, if any) + Interest Earned (if any)

= Cash Flow Before Taxes

Example: $12,013 – $8,589 = $3,424

7. Taxable Income (or Loss): This is the net operating income, less interest, depreciation of real property and capital improvements, and loan costs, plus interest earned on property bank accounts. Taxable income may be negative or positive. If it is negative (a loss), it can shelter the investor's other earnings and result in a negative tax liability on the investor's income tax return.

Formula:

Net Operating Income – Interest Paid – Depreciation – Amortization + Interest Earned
= Taxable Income or Loss

Example: $12,013 – $6,169 – $3,735 = $2,109

8. Tax Liability (Savings): This is the taxable income (or loss) times the tax bracket of the property owner.

Example: $2,109 × 30% = $633

9. Cash Flow After Taxes (CFAT): This is the amount of cash generated from the property after taxes have been considered. This figure is calculated by subtracting the tax liability from cash flow before taxes. It is the measure that determines the ability of the property to generate cash flow through its operations.

Formula:

Cash Flow Before Taxes – Tax Liability = Cash Flow After Taxes

Example: $3,424 – $633 = $2,791

10. Gross Rent Multiplier (GRM): This calculation provides a simple way to estimate the market value of any income-producing property. It is the ratio of the price of the property to its annual rental income before expenses such as property taxes, insurance, utilities, and maintenance (see operating expenses).

Formula:

Price / Gross Scheduled Income = GRM

Example: $120,000 / $20,400 Potential Annual Gross Income = 5.9% GRM

11. Capitalization Rate: The Cap Rate (as it is more commonly called) is the rate at which you discount future income to determine its present value. It is used to estimate the potential return on the investment. This figure is calculated by dividing the net operating income by the proposed asking price. The higher the Cap Rate is, the better it is for the buyer (lower purchase price). The lower the Cap Rate, the better it is for the seller (higher asking price).

Formula:

NOI / Value = Cap Rate

Example: $12,013/ $120,000 = 10.0%

12. Cash on Cash Return (COC): This represents the ratio of the property's annual cash flow (usually the first year before taxes) to the amount of the initial capital investment (down payment, loan fees, and acquisition costs). It is a very important ratio to evaluate the long-term performance of a property investment. You can compare the COC to the annual return on a certificate of deposit.

Formula:

Cash Flow Before Taxes (CFBT) / Capital Investment = Cash on Cash

Example: $3,424 / $27,600 = 12.4%

13. Operating Expense Ratio (OER): This represents the ratio of the property's total operating expenses to its gross operating income (GOI). The operating expense ratio is a useful tool for comparing the expenses of similar properties.

A reasonable OER should fall between 30% and 45%. If a piece of property has an unusually high OER, an investor should view this as a red flag to look deeper into why expenses are so much higher for this property than for comparable properties. Perhaps maintenance expenses are unusually high, for example.

Formula:

Operating Expenses / GOI = Operating Expense Ratio

Example: $6,347 / $18,360 = 34.6%

14. Debt Coverage Ratio (DCR), also known as Debt Service Coverage Ratio (DSCR): This is the ratio of the property's net operating income to its annual debt service for the year. A DCR of 1 indicates that the income is just sufficient to cover debt service payments (not a good situation). A DCR of less than 1 indicates that the property is unable to generate enough income to cover its payments.

A property with a DCR of 1.25 generates 1.25 times as much annual income as the annual debt service on the property. The greater the DCR is above 1.2, the more favorably it is viewed by lenders because this means the property generates more than enough income to repay the debt service. The higher the DCR, the better. Lenders typically require a DCR of 1.2 or more.

Factors that can affect the DCR may include such things as interest rate, down payment, vacancy rates in the area, oversupply of properties, current economic outlook, overall demand for real estate, physical condition and location of the property, age, crime rate in the area, proximity to shopping and schools, property management, overall upkeep, and so on.

On another note, lenders are now starting to use what is called a global DCR. This is a ratio that combines an investment portfolio of properties with weak cash flow or lower Cap Rates so that the buyer will be able to qualify for a commercial loan.

Formula:

Net Operating Income / Annual Debt Service = Debt Coverage Ratio

Example: $12,013 / $8,589 = 1.4

15. Break-Even Ratio (BER): This ratio measures the amount of money going out against the amount of money coming in, and it tells the investor what part of gross operating income will be used by all estimated expenses.

Lenders use the break-even ratio as one of their analysis methods when considering an investor's application for a loan. A high break-even ratio is a red flag that tells the lender that a property might be vulnerable to defaulting on its debt if the rental income declines.

The BER always must be less than 100% for an investment to be viable (the lower, the better). Lenders typically require a BER of 85% or less.

Formula:

Operating Expenses + Debt Service / Gross Operating Income = BER

Example: ($6,347 + $8,589) / $18,360 = 81.4%

16. Loan to Value (LTV): This is the ratio of the loan amount to the appraised value of the property. It measures the percentage of the property's appraised value or selling price that will be financed by the loan. A higher LTV means greater leverage for the investor (higher financial risk for the lender). A lower LTV means less leverage for the investor (lower financial risk for the lender).

Formula:

Loan Amount / Less of Appraised Value or Selling Price = LTV

17. Return on Investment (ROI) with Appreciation: This figure considers the four benefits of investing in real estate: income, principal reduction, appreciation, and depreciation. This measure will let you know how the potential investment compares against other properties that are under consideration.

Formula:

[Cash Flow Before Taxes (CFBT) + Principal Reduction –

Taxes Paid + Appreciation Estimate] / Cash Invested = Return on Investment with Appreciation

Example: ($3,424 + $2,420 – $633 + $2,400) / $27,600 = 27.6%

18. Return on Investment (ROI) without Appreciation: This figure considers three of the four benefits of investing in real estate: income, principal reduction, and depreciation. This measure will let you know how the potential investment compares against other properties that are under consideration.

Formula:

Cash Flow Before Taxes + Principal Reduction – Taxes Paid / Cash Invested = Return on Investment without Appreciation

Example: ($3,424 + $2,420 – $633) / $27,600 = 18.9%

19. Annual Debt Service (ADS): This is the total amount paid on the loan (interest payments and principal) over the course of one year.

How to use these formulas

The formulas discussed in this chapter should help you identify profitable investments and make good investment decisions when choosing among different properties. You will need to decide what level of results will allow you to accomplish your goals. Keep in mind that investors have different goals and objectives, so what may be good for another investor may not be good for you, or vice-versa.

Although these formulas may seem a bit overwhelming at first, I promise you that making these calculations is not rocket science. When you gain some practice applying them, you will be amazed at how useful they are.

You now have the power to analyze properties to determine whether a property is likely to be a good or bad investment. Using these formulas will help you identify and minimize risk.

Using these formulas will help you determine what a property is worth. Keep in mind that when you are evaluating a property it should be for the first year only. We cannot accurately predict what the future holds for the property because there are too many variables involved, such as increases or decreases in property assessments, changes in rental rates depending on the local market situation, unexpected expenses, and changes in your personal tax situation. All of these factors and others may affect the return that a property will generate.

You should not go at this alone. Having a residential investment specialist on your team is essential, and they should help you analyze any property you are considering purchasing. Their input will be a key factor in achieving your wealth building objective.

Key points to remember:

- ✓ Become familiar with various financial measures so you can determine whether a property under consideration will meet your financial objectives.
- ✓ You should base your decisions on whether the property will make money for you, not whether the property appeals to you emotionally. Remember that successful investors always fall in love with the deal rather than the property.
- ✓ Having a gut feeling that a property will be a good deal is not enough; you need to run the numbers even if you are not a "numbers person."
- ✓ Some of the information you require for evaluating a property's investment potential will be easy to find, while other types of information will be harder to track down.

Chapter 10

FLIP OR HOLD?

Have you ever flipped a property?

If your answer is "Yes," congratulations! If your answer is "No," you are probably wondering how to decide whether to flip or hold a specific property.

If your agent has experience with flipping and holding, they can explain how to make this decision. Remember, an agent should be able to bring you the value and expertise you deserve. Liking and trusting them is not enough. They must be able to tell you whether a specific property is likely to be a good flipper or a better rental. They should also show you how to figure out how much money you can expect to make on an average flip. The good, better, best spreadsheet described in this chapter will be a big help here.

The most important question to ask yourself is whether it is better for you to buy and hold a property or flip it. Did you know that if you flip a property in less than one year the profit is considered ordinary income and will be taxed as short-term capital gains based on your taxable income? However, if you buy and hold the property as a rental for longer than one year, you can benefit from a reduced tax rate on your profits because it is considered long-term capital gains. It is best to always consult your accountant concerning the potential tax consequences before deciding whether to flip or hold.

Flipping brings both rewards and challenges

Flipping houses has been extremely lucrative for me personally, so I find it easy to understand why more and more people are getting involved in flipping.

As the demand for properties with flipping potential has gone up, the supply has gone down. Competition among buyers has increased in recent years. The days of finding steals are long gone, and even my long-term clients who made serious money in 2005–2006 have been feeling the challenges. I am certain that you will face similar challenges in your area, making it even more critical to have the right agent on your side.

Why are fewer properties available for flipping now than in the past? Mainly because foreclosures are way down. This is good for the economy, and it's the main reason the real estate market has seen a nice turnaround.

The norm now is for potential buyers to pay higher prices and to contend with competing offers. This is not a bad thing, because it means the selling price will be higher after a property has been improved.

Today's increasingly competitive flipping environment is proof that real estate has withstood economic downturns and proven itself to be one of the best options for hard-working people to earn money and build wealth. I have made an average of $15,000 to $20,000 personally on each flip before taxes, and I have clients who make much more. How much do you need to make to make it worthwhile for you? I have a client that made over $300,000 in one year from flipping properties.

Why has flipping become so popular? Here are a couple of possible reasons:

1. Warren Buffett, the "Oracle of Omaha" and one of the richest men in America, told reporters in 2012 that if there was a practical way for him to purchase "a couple hundred thousand single-family homes" and manage them, he would do it.

2. TV shows have made the flipping process seem easy: You find a cheap property, put some money and sweat equity into fixing it up, and then you resell the house for a huge profit.

It is true that experienced real estate investors can make enormous profits by flipping. Even though inventories are way down, this is still a great time to get into the flipping game or to start building wealth by purchasing income-producing properties.

If you have thought about flipping but never pulled the trigger, now is the time to do it. If you have dabbled in real estate unsuccessfully in the past, now is the time to get re-engaged and apply the knowledge you are gaining from reading this book.

If you would like to start flipping, ask your agent to find you a property that has good potential as a "flipper." Although you can be successful finding properties on your own, it may seem like you are looking for the perfect piece of corn in the field. That's why it's so important to align yourself with a knowledgeable and experienced real estate agent. They have their finger on the pulse of the local market and will know when a good deal comes up, maybe even before it gets listed.

I started flipping properties in the 1980s before the term "flipping" was widely used. Flipping has been a very large part of my income, so I understand the ins and outs of this game. Keep in mind that I did not do any of the work to fix up these properties myself. On occasion, I even sold a few properties without doing anything at all to them. I made $10,000 simply by wholesaling—passing on the deal to a flipper or to someone who wanted to fix up the property and earn rental income.

I bought a property in late 2017 because it had five garages that I needed for storage. I wanted to get a separate legal description so that I could keep the garages and sell the building. Unfortunately, the city did not allow me to do that and I did not need or want another rental, so I sold the property a few months later and made $90,000 before paying taxes to Uncle Sam.

At this point you may be wondering whether I or other agents will compete with you for properties. The answer is NO. Many times, I have shown clients a property and they decided not to buy it for one reason or another, so I ended up purchasing it myself.

I have continued to flip properties for ordinary income and to rely on my sizable rental portfolio for wealth building and retirement income. Real estate investors often have strong opinions about whether it is better to buy and flip or buy and hold, but I have found that both strategies can produce excellent results. The best choice is the one that fulfills the investor's needs.

Have you talked with anyone lately who is not a fan of real estate? What was their opinion on flipping or long-term rentals? If they tried one of these strategies and it didn't work well for them, perhaps they made a poor decision or worked with a real estate agent who lacked experience with investment properties. Or maybe they were speculators rather than investors. Did they have a business plan? Did they pay too much to purchase a property or to remodel it and end up losing money? Investors can minimize the risk involved in flipping if they follow a business plan and make their money when they buy.

To me, flipping is like being an artist who takes a blank canvas and creates a beautiful painting. There is nothing more rewarding than reconditioning a rundown property and helping to improve the neighborhood.

Even more rewarding is the fact that you are making the dream of homeownership possible for a family and at the same time earning a nice profit. It's an example of the Win-Win concept at work.

I am often asked whether it's a better option to flip or to hold properties. My answer is that it depends on the investor's needs and objectives. Flipping is a terrific way to make a living, while buying and holding rental property is a great way to build wealth for the future. Both options are certainly better than doing nothing at all.

I think doing some of both is the best way to go—flipping for ordinary income and holding long-term rentals to build wealth. I don't think it is the best strategy to flip with the intent to use the profits to purchase another property that you intend on flipping. If you do this, your profits will be considered ordinary income and taxed accordingly.

A better option is to refinance the property and try to pull out most of your investment. If you decide not to keep it the property as a long term rental, keep it for over a year and pay the capital gains tax. Do you need the money now, or would you be better off building wealth and retirement income?

Advantages of flipping

1. The main advantage of flipping is that a nice profit can be made in a relatively short period of time. As I have said in

previous chapters, the key to success is not to overpay for the property or to underestimate the work required. It is critical to stay on budget and to complete the project on schedule. Most projects should be completed in three to six weeks.

2. When you flip properties, you are your own boss. You can reap the financial rewards of your decisions. If flipping is done correctly, it can easily replace your income from the workplace.

3. For people who are in another line of work, flipping can provide an additional source of income.

4. Flipping is available to anyone who is creditworthy and has a solid financial statement. There are few other investment options available in which substantial amounts of money can be made in a relatively short period of time, especially for those who have limited financial resources.

Disadvantages of flipping

The only significant disadvantage of flipping is the risk of losing money, but any worthwhile venture involves risk. No risk, no reward. Money can be found on the other side of fear. You can minimize risk and increase your chances of success by working with the right agent who can help you predict the anticipated expenses and purchase the property at a price that makes sense. Your agent can help you explore different scenarios. For example, if the property is purchased at a certain price and sold at a certain price (less the remodeling expenses, carrying costs, etc.), will you make the desired profit?

Although there are always risks involved in anything we may do, I believe the benefits of flipping greatly outweigh the disadvantages and I would strongly recommend it for anyone who is looking to make extra money or even establish it as an ongoing business venture. I have found that one of the keys to success is using the good, better, best spreadsheet described below.

The good, better, best scenario

Flipping is often portrayed as a complicated process by people who write books, do seminars, and charge people substantial fees to buy their systems. Maybe you know someone who attended a flipping seminar and ended up spending thousands of dollars on information that was not necessary. Or maybe they hired a coach or mentor who didn't even live in their community. In either case, they were spending money that could have been put to better use for a down payment or remodeling costs.

In talking with my clients about how to evaluate investment property, I always suggest that they envision three different scenarios for profit potential: good, better, and best.

A. The good price point is the highest price you should pay for the property and the lowest price it can be sold for to make what you consider a good profit. For example, a property may have a purchase price of $80,000 and a selling price of $130,000, and the total expenses for repairs, selling costs, etc., are $30,000, producing a profit of $20,000 before taxes. How many hourly wage earners do you know who must work for three to four months to earn $20,000?

B. The better price point is the price you should pay for the property and the price it can be sold for to make what you consider a better profit. Example: $75,000 purchase price, $135,000 selling price, $30,000 total expenses for repairs, selling costs, etc., producing $30,000 profit before taxes. How many hourly wage earners do you know who must work for five to eight months to earn $30,000?

C. The best price point is the lowest price you could pay for the property and the highest price it could be sold for to make what you consider the best possible profit. Example: $70,000 purchase price, $140,000 selling price, $30,000 total expenses for repairs, selling costs, etc., producing $40,000 profit before taxes. How many hourly wage earners do you know who must work a year or more to earn $40,000?

Planning is the most effective way to minimize risk. What if the property doesn't sell? This outcome is unlikely when you have these three scenarios in mind, but a property that doesn't sell can also become a rental unit. Instant equity is the result, and wealth building is the long-term outcome.

Holding on to a property for a longer period has an additional benefit: the profit will be taxed at a lower rate. When a property is sold within the first year after purchase, the IRS treats the profit as ordinary income and taxes it at rates that can be very high, depending on your income tax bracket. If the property is held for more than one year after being purchased, the profits made by selling it are considered capital gains and are taxed at a rate that is typically lower than for ordinary income.

As with any other aspect of real estate investment, people who are contemplating flipping properties or owning rental properties should seek the advice of a competent and knowledgeable accountant and of course a real estate agent who has flipped and held properties.

Selling time

Flipping should happen within a relatively short period of time. The longer a property is on the market, the less the profit will be because the investor is responsible for paying utilities, insurance, carrying costs, and so on until the property is sold.

Capital requirement

Although some people will say that a disadvantage of flipping is that you need a large amount of money to purchase and upgrade a property, I do not see it as a disadvantage at all. Anyone who is creditworthy can secure funds. Cash is always best, but investors can use other people's money (OPM) by opening a line of credit, taking out a bridge loan, or pooling resources with a partner. Earning money through flipping doesn't have to be a fantasy. It is a reality for me and for the clients I serve.

Advantages of holding

Holding onto a rental property over the long term is an excellent way to build wealth. While your tenant reduces the debt, property values continue to go up and residual income for your retirement years is the outcome.

How should you decide whether to buy and flip or buy and hold? Consider the following questions:

1. What are you planning to do with the profits? Do you want to buy a car, take a vacation, pay off debt, pay for your children's college tuition, or use the funds for a down payment on your next flip or rental property?

2. Are you aware that your profits from flipping will be treated as ordinary income and taxes will have to be paid?

3. Is it better for you to earn income now (flipping) or residual income later (buy and hold)?

4. Are you aware that if you use the profits to buy another flip, your profits will be treated as ordinary income and you will pay much higher taxes than what you would pay on capital gains if you rented the property and kept it for at least a year?

My system for flipping properties is no different from that used for purchasing properties to hold for rental purposes; however, I believe you should not hesitate to pay more for a long-term rental property because of the power of leverage and the fact that ultimately the tenant is making your mortgage payment. Think about it: borrowing an additional $10,000 at 5% interest on a 15-year loan will cost you an extra $39.54 per month. Will the rent cover this?

Flipping is all about the bottom line: Will the property bring you enough money to make the project worthwhile? I have successfully flipped many properties using the good, better, best scenario and the remodeling estimator instead of wasting my money on costly systems.

My system for flipping a property:

1. **Find** a property with investment potential.

2. **Analyze** the property. If it is a single-family dwelling, comparables are the best indicator of the property's value after it has been fixed up. If it's a multi-unit, more information is needed to run the numbers. If the property passes this test, the next step is to write an offer.

3. **Buy** the right property that meets your needs and objectives.

4. **Fix** the property. Make repairs and/or updates to get optimum rents or profits. Be sure to stay on budget and on schedule.

5. **Flip** quickly.

Step 1. Find a property with investment potential

If a property is truly a great deal, you must act quickly before it is gone. Keep in mind that you are competing with other investors for limited properties that are available. Choose a potential purchase based on numbers, not emotions. Will the property meet your financial objectives? If you pay too much for a property or spend considerably more for the rehab than your budgeted amount, your desired profit may not become a reality. In other words, fall in love with the deal rather than with the property.

How to recognize a good deal

This is where your agent can bring tremendous value if they know how to analyze investment properties. Real estate agents who are also investors and flippers bring knowledge that only comes with experience, research, and education.

Knowing what a good deal is should not be left up to chance. Is a $50,000 or $100,000 property a good deal to flip? To find out you will need the following information:

1. What are comparable properties selling for in the same neighborhood?

2. What is the expected selling price?

3. What are the expected repair costs and other expenses?

4. What is the expected profit?

5. Based on the above information, is the project worth doing?

Where to find properties

Although there are many ways to find properties for investment purposes, my top choice is the Multiple Listing Service (MLS) at www.mls.com. As I have mentioned, the competition is quite fierce for properties with investment potential. However, on any given day you can find properties that will meet your criteria.

I search the MLS probably four to five times a day for new listings, price reductions, and so on, which increases the likelihood of finding properties that meet my clients' criteria.

I network with other real estate agents (not just those who are affiliated with my company). I let them know that I have potential buyers for properties that need work. You may wonder why another agent would tell me about these types of properties. The main reason likely is that they don't have investor clients.

If you want to find properties on your own, you can also place ads in the real estate section of your local newspaper saying that you buy properties that need work, estate sales, and so on. Avoid gimmicks like claiming that you will buy houses in any condition if that is not your intent. Look in the rental section of your newspaper, especially in the multi-unit section, and you may find ads for properties that meet your criteria.

Step 2. Analyze a property

The most important criterion for a potential flipper is the financial component. Your offer should be based on analyzing whether the property is likely to produce the desired level of profits. At this stage of the process, you will need to decide whether you are comfortable writing an offer. If the deal doesn't make sense financially, it will not be a good property to flip.

Keep in mind that you can make an offer that is subject to inspection by a contractor to determine whether remodeling costs are satisfactory to you. The earnest deposit can even be submitted upon removal of the inspection when you are satisfied with your due diligence. At the buying stage, a more detailed analysis is conducted.

It is important to know what factors contribute to the value of a property. For example, kitchens and baths are the basics in upgrading a property. Look at comparable properties to find out what the property is likely to sell for when it is fixed up.

Step 3. Buy the right property that meets your needs and objectives

Everything that needs to happen from the purchase agreement to closing takes place in step 3.

At this stage it is also important to do whatever due diligence is desired. This may include inspections by contractor(s) to determine whether the remodeling costs are satisfactory to you. Due diligence can be a useful out because "satisfactory" will have a different meaning for each person. Are you comfortable with all the findings? If the property is a multi-unit rather than a single-family dwelling, the same due diligence may apply.

Depending on whether the property meets your criteria, the offer is either written or not. If the property will be used as a rental, you may be able to pay more than you could pay for a property that is purchased as a flipper.

How will the offer be written? Keep in mind that the preferred method of acquiring these types of properties is cash. Making an offer that is subject to a loan is still possible, but there is a very good chance that other buyers will offer cash for the property. Cash offers are viewed favorably by sellers because they don't involve appraisals or underwriting guidelines.

Other options for making cash offers include using a line of credit (which is still considered a cash offer) or bridge loan (also considered a cash offer). The credit line or bridge loan may be secured by collateral such as your personal residence, securities, or other assets.

You can also use funds from your self-directed or Roth IRA to purchase properties. A self-directed IRA is the lesser known of IRA options and requires account owners to make active investments on behalf of the plan. To open a self-directed or Roth IRA, the owner of the account must hire a trustee or custodian to hold the IRA assets and be responsible for administering the account and filing the required documents with the IRS. For additional information about using IRAs to purchase investment properties, see Chapter 14.

Many real estate agents and investors are getting frustrated because it is becoming harder to find "deals." However, the fact that deals are harder to find today doesn't mean that no deals are available. In addition, when property values are higher you may pay more for a property, but it also means that rents are going up and so are the prices that you will receive for flipped properties.

The real estate market has changed from what it was like a few years ago. Likely low-ball offers are just a waste of time. A better strategy is to ask your agent to write an offer where you would pay a certain amount (such as $500) more than the next-highest offer up to a certain maximum amount. With this strategy, the agent must be able to verify the next-highest offer. This strategy does not work well with foreclosures.

Step 4. Fix up the property

After buying a property, the next step is to make repairs and/or updates to bring optimum profits. Keeping the project on budget during this phase is key.

Although you may have an opportunity to purchase a property in a good neighborhood that doesn't need any repairs, owner-occupied buyers are likely to make higher offers than you are willing to make for this type of property.

Based on my experience, the properties that owner-occupied buyers walk away from are those that need work and sometimes even major reconstruction. These types of properties offer the best opportunities for investors.

Some investors will walk away from certain properties that involve major remodeling tasks, but there are investors for every type of property. Some may consider re-roofing, a new furnace, bathroom, or foundation to be a major project while others may think nothing of such repairs.

Will an inexperienced investor who has no construction knowledge make an offer on a property that is a major project? Probably not.

I have shown the same property to different investors, and some have passed on it while one has ended up buying a great property that met their criteria.

Investors have different needs and objectives. Some may only want to do minor repairs to just get by and probably will not make much profit as a flipper. Other investors may be willing to take the property to a higher level. For example, one investor might paint the kitchen cabinets without replacing the original countertops, while another might install new cabinets, countertops, and so on. The outcome of more remodeling most likely will be higher profit for the flipper.

Taking things to the next level makes sense only if a property is a good deal. There is no need to buy the property if it would involve so much remodeling that you would end up paying the retail price. Keep in mind that the objective is to make money, not to break even.

What is a reasonable amount to spend on repairs or remodeling? The numbers should provide some direction.

For example, let's say you have purchased a $60,000 property with $15,000 in repair costs for a total investment of $75,000.

Comparable properties in the same neighborhood sell in the $110,000 range and you bought this property to flip. Carrying costs and selling expenses are $12,000, for a total investment of $87,000.

The potential profit in this deal is $23,000 less tax consequences—not a bad return in just a few short months. You can pay back the line of credit you used for the down payment and then move on to the next deal.

Flipping strategies

What steps should you take to improve the property before putting it on the market?

Keep in mind that most of the remodeling budget should be

devoted to updating the kitchen and bath(s). Does that mean you should install granite counters instead of Formica? It depends on the price point.

What about replacing kitchen cabinets versus painting? Again, it depends on the price point of the expected sale.

Remodeling does not have to be expensive. It is not necessary to hire a high-end contractor who is likely to make more money than you do.

You should focus on making improvements that will increase the overall appeal of the property as well as its market value, thereby increasing the profit margin.

If your remodeling efforts will cost $25,000 and the value of the property will only increase by $18,000, then perhaps this would be a better wholesaling project than a flipper. You can sell the property to another investor and make money without doing anything to it. On the other hand, if the remodeling cost will be $18,000 and it will increase the value of the property by $25,000, then the fix-up project should move forward. There is no reason to spend $1 to make $1. Spending 50 cents to make $1 makes a lot more sense.

You must weigh the remodeling costs (including time and effort) against the potential for profit. If the project will make the property more appealing to a potential buyer and not cut into the profit, then it may be a great way to make a nice return on the property investment.

The best way to improve home values without overspending is to do exactly what needs doing and nothing more. Making the necessary improvements will increase the property's value and make it more attractive to a buyer.

There are numerous simple things an investor can do to increase the value of a property:

1. Pay attention to curb appeal. A good first impression can dramatically increase the value of the property.
2. Take care of landscaping and yard work (mowing, trimming, and weeding). The yard is the first thing potential buyers will see. Planting flowers is an inexpensive way to make a property more appealing.
3. Remove old carpet and refinish hardwood floors.
4. Refinish or reface kitchen cabinets and replace knobs. Replace lighting fixtures in the kitchen ceiling.
5. Paint interior/exterior.
6. Remodel bathroom(s).

Step 5. Flip quickly

Ideally, the agent who lists the property should be the one who helped you buy it. Your agent will make a commission on the sale and look forward to working with you again.

To flip quickly, the listing price should be lower than the asking price for similar properties in the same neighborhood. As an investor, you should look at the bottom line and not be emotional in making these decisions. A few thousand dollars plus or minus is not a big issue.

By contrast, owner-occupied sellers tend to be more emotional in their expectations. Their property may need updating, yet they want the buyer to pay a premium price. If you are offering a similar property in better condition for less money, buyers are likely to choose it instead. I like to tell my clients, "Let those properties help sell yours."

Key points to remember:

- ✓ Flipping has become more popular while foreclosed properties have become harder to find, but good deals are still available.
- ✓ Flipping can allow you to make a substantial profit within a relatively short period of time, while owning rental property will help you build wealth over the long term. Doing both strategies is a good option.
- ✓ The IRS treats profits from short-term flipping (within a year of purchase) as ordinary income. If a property is held for more than a year before being sold, the profits are considered capital gains and taxed at a lower rate.
- ✓ To determine the potential profit from flipping a property, you must run the numbers.
- ✓ Don't go overboard in remodeling a property. Establish a budget and stick to it.

Chapter 11

PROPERTY MANAGEMENT

Most likely you will choose to manage your own investment portfolio, but if your time is in short supply you may choose to delegate most of the hands-on tasks to a property management company.

Real estate investors have different needs and objectives. Hourly wage earners invest in real estate to receive income from flipping or rentals. By contrast, high-income individuals often pay far more than their fair share of taxes, and real estate investing can help lighten their tax burden. They are often short on time and will be more likely to invest in real estate if they can hire a property management company to handle the day-to-day tasks of property ownership.

The role of a property management company is like that of a stockbroker or financial planner. For a fee, they manage their client's portfolio. Investors should not hesitate to hire a property management company because the advantages are substantial.

A property management company has a primary responsibility to the landlord and a secondary responsibility to the tenant. They play a crucial role in fulfilling the expectations of both parties to the lease, since both parties have specific rights and benefits.

Hiring a competent and reputable property management company will go a long way toward ensuring a positive experience. This type of help is well worth the additional expense involved.

Keep in mind that property managers are businesslike and unemotional in doing their job. They don't get chummy with the tenants. They are friendly and cordial, but they treat all tenants the same. They can keep the investor out of trouble because they understand the landlord-tenant laws.

What are some of the ways a property management company can help you?

1. Generally they attract higher-quality tenants because they do the proper background screening, from landlord verifications to criminal checks. Of course, nothing is 100% guaranteed and a perfectly qualified tenant can eventually become a bad tenant. However, a property management company tends to have a better overall outcome regarding tenants.

2. An experienced property management company regularly reviews hundreds of applications, so they have the expertise to quickly screen candidates and recognize warning signs. Any experienced landlord will tell you that it takes only one bad tenant to create costly legal fees and a financial burden.

3. The property management company is knowledgeable about the latest landlord-tenant laws. State laws cover many aspects of the landlord-tenant relationship, from security deposits to evictions and rules about landlord access to rental property. A summary of the state laws can be found at http://www.nolo.com/legal-encyclopedia/

state-landlord-tenant-laws

4. Property managers also understand the mandates of the Occupational Safety and Health Administration (OSHA), Environmental Protection Agency (EPA), Americans with Disabilities Act (ADA), Fair Housing and Equal Opportunity (FHEO), and the Equal Employment Opportunity Commission (EEOC). They are well worth the expense because avoiding one lawsuit will more than pay the annual fees charged by a property management company.

5. *When* you a hire a *property manager, you ensure anonymity* between you and the renter. The property manager will be the point of contact with your tenant for all matters involving the rental. In other words, the property manager will handle every detail and keep you informed. An effective property manager will put a wall between you and any potentially uncomfortable situations.

When you are analyzing a potential investment property, be sure to include property management fees of 6 to 10% even if you intend to manage the property. What happens if you need to move out of town unexpectedly due to a job transfer or you discover that you don't enjoy dealing directly with tenants?

Sometimes the additional expense of a property manager makes the difference between positive and negative cash flow from an investment. However, hiring a property management company can still make sense because of the equity associated with owning the property.

Although a majority of "Ma and Pa" investors will manage their own portfolios, for other investors one of the biggest decisions they must make will be whether to use a property management company. In my case, I felt that my time would be better utilized by focusing on my work as a real estate agent than by handling all of the day-to-day responsibilities of being a landlord. One small commission check covers the property management fees.

What does a property management company do?

First and foremost, property managers deal directly with prospects and tenants. Additional services provided by property management companies include the following:

1. Leasing
2. Maintenance and repairs
3. Rent collection
4. Lease renewals
5. Record keeping
6. Payments
7. Responding to complaints
8. Evictions

Leasing

Property managers take care of everything related to ensuring that a rental property is continuously occupied, from advertising the property to conducting background checks on prospective tenants.

They know the best methods to advertise, improve, and prepare the property to be rented. They market the property and charge a finder's fee when they find a tenant—typically half a month or a full month's rent.

Property managers know the local rental market and will set the monthly rent accordingly. Rents that are too high could increase the time required to line up a tenant, and rents that are too low will ultimately reduce the investor's income. The property manager may choose to rent the property for a higher amount than the investor would have charged on their own. Higher rental income ultimately makes the investment worth more.

Maintenance and repairs

Property managers coordinate all aspects of maintenance, from preparing the property for a new tenant to handling general repairs, plumbing, HVAC, and re-keying the locks. They are available 24/7 to deal with emergency situations. They can also oversee major remodeling jobs.

Rent collection: The property management company is responsible for making sure tenants pay their rent on time. They understand that collecting the rent on time is vital to your livelihood and essential for making mortgage payments on schedule. The company's methods of handling rent collection or late payments could make the difference between your success and failure as an investor.

I have seen many inexperienced or weak landlords who were manipulated by their tenants. By contrast, property managers establish expectations for tenants and enforce the terms of the lease.

Lease renewals: Property managers find out in advance whether a tenant is planning to renew the lease or move out when it expires. If the lease will not be renewed, they will show the property (assuming it is in showable condition) to prospective tenants so that a new tenant can move in quickly and minimize the loss of rent due to vacancy.

Record keeping: The property management company will keep you informed on a monthly basis about your property's income and expenses. They will also issue a detailed annual report that you can give to your accountant.

Payments: Property managers make payments on your behalf, ranging from monthly mortgage payments to utility bills.

Responding to complaints: A competent property manager responds promptly to tenants' complaints. A happy tenant stays longer than one who is dissatisfied, and tenant retention will maximize your rental income.

Evictions: There is a right and wrong way to evict tenants who violate the terms of the lease. Noncompliance with tenant/landlord laws during the eviction process can create major problems for investors. Property managers understand how to handle evictions to achieve the best possible outcome.

Questions to ask a property management company

It's important to understand that property management companies are not all the same, just as real estate agents are not all the same.

A good property management company will help you have a successful experience. Their knowledge and experience can give you the peace of mind that comes from knowing that your property is in good hands.

The experience level of a property management company is a key factor in achieving a good outcome. To evaluate a company before choosing to work with them, be sure to ask the following questions:

1. How many properties do you manage?
2. How long have you been in business?
3. Have you had any complaints from the state real estate commission?
4. How long does it take, on average, for you to rent a property?
5. What are your fees, and what services are provided?
6. Do you have your own employees who do the work, or do you use vendors? Is there an additional premium for the vendors, and if so, how much is it?
7. How do you handle evictions, and what happens with money that is owed? Do you turn over the debt to a collection agency? If so, what fees are charged?

You will always have the option of managing your own properties and not having to pay a fee to someone else, but you might want to think about how much your time is worth. If you are a high-income professional, you may find that it's much more cost-effective to hire a property management company than to handle everything yourself. In my own case, I believe it makes sense to leave the day-to-day duties to the experts.

Advantages and disadvantages of using a property management company

There are pros and cons involved in using a property management company to deal with the day-to-day aspects of being a landlord.

Disadvantages

Probably the main disadvantage of hiring a property management company is the effect on the property's bottom line. The average property management company will initially charge half a month to one month's rent to line up a new tenant. They will charge 6% to 10% of each month's rent after that, depending on the services they provide.

The initial property management fee covers their expense for any advertising, showing the property, processing an applicant, verifying credit, and other general expenses that come with setting up a new account.

When you are analyzing a property to decide whether it will be a good investment, it is imperative to include property management expenses in your calculations. You need find out whether the property will cash flow with the additional fees.

Advantages

Given the duties and responsibilities already mentioned, hiring a property management company is worth the expense for some investors. For them, the advantages of using a property management company far outweigh the disadvantages. Even if the numbers are tight it is still worth it.

Remember that real estate investors make their money when they buy. In that regard, the properties you purchase should be good deals so that instant equity starts from day one. Does it make sense to buy a property that offers immediate equity and hire a property management company to manage it? Of course it does.

Personally, I would rather take advantage of all the benefits my career in real estate has to offer and utilize the services of a competent property management company to handle the day-to-day tasks involved in being a landlord. You may eventually reach the same conclusion.

Key points to remember:

- ✓ Do you have what it takes to deal with the day-to-day responsibilities of owning a rental property? If not, property management is an excellent option if the property will still cash flow.
- ✓ If you are a high-income individual or do not have the time to manage your own property, you should explore the possibility of working with a property management company.
- ✓ Property management companies can provide a wide range of services hassle-free.
- ✓ Property managers can improve tenant retention by responding promptly to complaints.
- ✓ The advantages of hiring a property management company are well worth the fees involved, particularly when it comes to avoiding lawsuits.
- ✓ The property manager is to real estate as the stockbroker/financial advisor is to your other investments.

Chapter 12

TYPES OF REAL ESTATE

As an investor, you should be aware of the different real estate options available so you can choose the one that will best serve your needs and objectives. The type of investment that is best for you will depend on your knowledge, experience, objectives, and risk tolerance.

The residential investment market will always hold the greatest appeal for many investors because these properties are relatively easy to find, acquire, and manage. Some investors are attracted to duplexes, fourplexes, or small to medium-sized apartments (under 24 units) and others to commercial properties.

As you know from previous chapters, my specialty is residential properties. My portfolio includes a variety of single-family dwellings and duplexes. I no longer own anything above a duplex, nor have I owned any commercial properties or large apartment buildings.

Keep in mind that there are real estate agents who specialize in each of the different types of properties. If the agent who is working with you doesn't have the knowledge you seek, ask him or her to recommend someone who does. I have always subscribed to the motto "Only do the things that you know." I believe it is best for the client to have an experienced and knowledgeable agent as the lead agent, so I have co-listed with other agents in the past.

Regardless of what types of properties one invests in, being a real estate investor is one of the greatest opportunities available for people who want to build wealth and have control over their financial future. There is no "Wall Street" or other outside influence that controls the financial future of real estate investors. You make your own decisions about everything from tenant selection to what type of real estate investment best suits you.

Below is a brief summary of the different types of real estate investments available, including residential, commercial, apartments, retail centers, hotels and motels, senior housing facilities, land development, golf courses, industrial properties, mixed-use properties, mobile home parks, and real estate investment trusts (REITs).

Residential properties

The "residential" category includes properties such as houses, townhomes, condos, duplexes, triplexes, fourplexes, and so on. Although duplexes and fourplexes are considered income-producing properties, they can be occupied by the owner, so they are considered residential properties. You can use an FHA loan to buy anything from a single-family residence to a fourplex if you use the property as your primary residence.

One of the greatest advantages of owning residential properties is that it requires a relatively small investment as a down payment and therefore this option is within reach of most people who want to get into the investment "game." This type of investment is ideal for the beginner or novice investor, as residential properties are relatively easy to rent.

Commercial properties

This category consists mostly of office buildings that vary in size, style, and purpose. These properties may be leased to small local businesses or rented to national chains.

Investing in the commercial market is not recommended for beginners because it requires much more sophistication and knowledge than the residential market and the risk is much greater.

On the positive side, commercial properties can provide excellent cash flow and stability due to leases that may last as long as 25 years, providing consistent income for the duration of the lease.

On the negative side, there is a lot of risk involved. Office building occupancy is highly sensitive to changing economic conditions. If these properties become vacant, it may take months or even years to find a new tenant. Meanwhile, the mortgage payment still must be made.

Small apartment buildings

These types of properties include everything from a five-unit building to one that has 50 units. The value of these types of properties is not based on comparables but rather on the income produced. This type of property is more difficult to finance than a residential property and will require a sizable down payment and different underwriting guidelines. Although small apartment buildings can provide significant cash flow, they require more day-to-day management than residential investments. Hiring a property management company is advisable for a beginning investor.

Although this type of property is not listed often, it may represent an excellent opportunity for some investors. If a building is rundown and underperforming, a savvy and knowledgeable investor can purchase it at a low price and raise its value by improving it, increasing the income, decreasing the expenses, and managing it personally or with the help of a property management company.

Large apartment complexes

This category encompasses very large complexes that often include a swimming pool, have a full-time, on-site management staff, and can cost in the millions of dollars. This type of property may be owned by a hedge fund or insurance company or it may be purchased through syndication (a process in which a group of individual investors pool their financial resources). Rarely is it owned by one individual.

Retail centers

This form of investment includes shopping malls, strip malls, neighborhood shopping centers, mega malls, storefronts, and so on. Many retail properties include a well-known anchor store that serves as the draw for shoppers. Leases for this type of property may include specialized language, such as stipulations that the landlord will receive a percentage of sales generated by the tenant in addition to monthly rent.

Hotel and motels

This type of investment combines real estate (buildings) and businesses (restaurants and retail shops) to generate revenue. This category isn't the best place for a novice investor to get started. Many experienced investors find it to be a fun and profitable area until they lose a lot of money. One way to get started in this niche is to buy the real estate and lease it to another company that will operate the facility. Running a hotel is a business in itself, not simply an investment, and running a business brings with it a whole new set of rules, regulations, and headaches.

Senior housing facilities

The three primary categories of senior housing facilities are independent living communities, assisted living communities, and nursing homes (also known as skilled nursing facilities). Continuing care retirement communities (CCRCs) generally provide all three housing types in one location, allowing residents to easily transition to higher levels of care as they age. Like a hotel or motel, a senior housing facility is a business as well as a building.

Land development

This category of commercial real estate is exciting because it can bring high rewards. However, the risk of failure also is high, and the outcome can painful if one jumps into land development without knowing what they are doing.

Golf courses

Are you interested in buying a golf course? Here's a web site that specializes in the sales of golf courses:

http://www.nationalgolfgroup.com/golf-courses-for-sale.cfm

According to a *Wall Street Journal* report, there are 16,000 golf courses with 18 or 36 holes, 4,500 courses with 9 holes, and fewer than 900 par 3 courses in the United States.

Industrial properties

Industrial real estate includes storage units, car washes, and other special-purpose real estate that generates income from customers who temporarily use the facility.

Although there are risks involved in this type of investment, research can reduce the likelihood of a negative outcome. For example, if you want to own a storage facility you should first research the number of storage facilities in your area, find out where they are located, and try to determine how full they are. Use phone book listings and Chamber of Commerce data to compile a list of competitors. You can make phone inquiries as a prospective renter to determine availability.

If you decide to invest in a storage facility, find a location that meets the objectives of your business plan. Units catering to businesses should be located near office parks or business centers. Personal units are best situated at the fringes of residential communities where renters can have easy and convenient access to their belongings. One benefit of owning and operating a storage facility is that tenants aren't going to call the owner at midnight to complain that their furnace broke down.

Mixed-use properties

An example of a mixed-use property might be a six-story building with retail space, a restaurant, or some other business on the first floor. The second and third floor could consist of individual offices. On the fourth floor a law firm might occupy the entire floor, and the fifth and sixth floors could be devoted to apartments or condos. Mixed-use properties are popular investments for those who have significant financial resources.

Mobile home parks

Mobile home parks (or manufactured home communities) are one of the few investment properties where the buyer can immediately begin receiving cash flow. As with the storage unit scenario, the investor owns the ground and any permanent buildings on the facility. Tenants are responsible for making repairs to their mobile homes.

Real estate investment trusts

Real estate investment trusts (REITs) trade like stocks. Each REIT consists of a group of investors who jointly own a portfolio of real property or real estate mortgages.

Types of net leases that may apply to some types of real property

Nonresidential properties often have net leases that define the responsibilities of the landlord and the tenant differently from residential leases. Three types of net leases are described below:

- ✓ *Single net or "N" leases:* The tenant pays the basic monthly rent plus property taxes. The landlord or property owner pays operating expenses (also known as common area maintenance, or CAM) and property insurance.
- ✓ *Double net lease (NN)* – The tenant agrees to pay a basic monthly rent as well as the property taxes and property insurance. The landlord is responsible for all other operating expenses.
- ✓ *Triple net lease (NNN)* – The tenant agrees to pay a basic monthly rent as well as property taxes, property insurance, and maintenance expenses.

Generally, single-tenant office buildings are leased on a triple net basis (NNN). This type of lease calls for the tenant to be responsible for all costs associated with occupancy.

Regardless of the type of property that is being considered, potential investors should seek the advice of a competent CPA and attorney before moving forward with the purchase of a property. These professionals can assist you in fulfilling the legal requirements involved and in establishing financial goals. Of significant importance is how you intend to purchase the property. Will it be in your name, as an LLC, with a self-directed IRA or Roth IRA? Your agent will help with the purchase. Your CPA, attorney, and property management company can help you with everything else.

In conclusion, always consider your exit plan when purchasing any type of property. Think about who would be the likely buyer of a property other than a residence, because a residence is much easier to sell and the likely buyer will be an owner-occupied buyer or a beginner investor. When you sell any property above a four-unit dwelling, the likely buyer will be another investor. Based on my experience, trying to have two investors agree on the value of a property is like pulling teeth—very painful. The seller would not buy the property for what he or she is asking, and the buyer thinks the property is not worth the price that the seller has set. The financials play a big role in determining the property's value, because the income and expenses will have a significant impact on what the property is worth.

Key points to remember:

- ✓ Many real estate investors specialize in residential properties because these properties are relatively easy to understand, find, acquire, manage, and sell.
- ✓ You should familiarize yourself with the various investment options that are available to you because at some point you may want to change your strategy and invest in other types of real estate.
- ✓ Different types of real estate come with varying levels of risk and rewards. Always keep in mind that if you ever want to sell your residential property, the likely buyer will be an owner-occupied buyer. With other investment options, the buyer will be another investor who will be much more sophisticated.

Chapter 13

TREATING REAL ESTATE AS A BUSINESS

Real estate investing is a business that should be taken seriously, no matter whether it is done on a part-time or full-time basis. In addition to writing a business plan, you will need to decide how you will hold ownership (if more than one person is involved in the business) and whether to operate as a sole proprietorship, partnership, or LLC (limited liability company). As with any other business, you will also need to have an exit plan.

What are the benefits of writing a business plan?

Writing a business plan can help you consider the details of your business, including aspects you may not have explored previously.

Looking at your business plan periodically can help you monitor whether you are on track to meet your short- and long-term goals. What do you want your business to look like one year, five years, and ten years down the road?

Another great reason to prepare a business plan is that it will help tremendously if you want to borrow money. Having a plan will show the lending institution that you are serious about investing in real estate and you intend to achieve success. Your business plan should be based on realistic expectations, not pie in the sky.

Although it may take some time and energy to prepare a business plan, it is well worth taking the time to do it right.

The plan must include clear descriptions of the types of property you will consider and the types you will walk away from.

Review: A, B, C, D classification of properties and areas

Along these lines, let's take another look at the A, B, C, D classification of properties that was introduced in Chapter 8. Although assigning these letter grades can sometimes feel more like an art than a science, the property classes are typically characterized by the following features:

1. "A" properties

These properties are like blue-chip stock. They tend to be newer properties built within the last five to fifteen years with the most up-to-date amenities. There is no deferred maintenance. Older properties in excellent condition that are in extremely desirable areas also can fall in this category, as can properties located near universities.

2. "B" properties

These properties may be a notch or two below an A property without the same amenities. They tend to be a bit older. They may have some deferred maintenance, and they usually have appreciation potential. The savvy investor can quickly raise the property's value by making minor improvements.

3. "C" properties

These are typically older properties built 30+ years ago with much fewer amenities. They may be a notch or two below a B. They may be in up-and-coming neighborhoods. They usually have more deferred maintenance. The savvy investor can quickly transform a C into a B by making minor improvements.

4. "D" properties

These properties are in undesirable areas. They may be in very poor condition and located in high-crime neighborhoods. The neighborhood is a bigger problem than the condition of the property, because properties can be updated but little can be done about the neighborhood. These properties may have a lot of deferred maintenance. Rents are low, and the quality of the tenant may not be great. Unless the neighborhood turns around there will probably be little or no appreciation. These properties require intense management and are not recommended for the brand-new investor. A lot of money is being made with "D" properties, and although they are cash flow machines, they require a lot of attention and repairs. These properties can be compared to penny stock.

Timing is everything. Your real estate agent should be knowledgeable about areas that are improving as well as areas that are declining. Depending on changes in the neighborhood, what may be a D property today could become a B property in a few years and vice versa.

When you evaluate areas, you can use a similar classification system:

A – Newer growth areas

B – Older, stable areas

C – Older, declining, or stable areas

D – Older, declining, potentially rapidly declining areas

These guidelines will help you to determine the property types and locations you are looking for, so you can share this information with your agent and include it in your business plan. The key is to identify enough of the right properties that will help you accomplish your investment goals.

In choosing a property, you should focus on properties in areas that are equal to or better than the class of the property itself (for example, a B property in a B or A area) and avoid properties in areas that are lower than the property class (for example, an A property in a C area). The area class you invest in will have a great deal of influence on the stability of your portfolio over time and will determine whether it appreciates or declines in value during periods of economic fluctuation. An A property will have a much harder time performing like an A property if it is in a C area, but a C property might perform better over time if it's in an A area.

If you are looking for investments with the highest appreciation potential and the best initial cash flow, you will want to look for A and B properties located in A and B areas or in the path of progress. You will want to avoid C properties in C areas. If you are not as interested in appreciation but are looking for investments with strong cash flow, then B and C properties in B and C areas would be the best fit.

Sample Business Plan

To give you a glimpse of the types of information that a business plan for a real estate investor should include, a sample business plan framework is included on the next few pages. You can use this example to create your own business plan. A filled-out business plan also is included in the Resources section near the end of this book.

Sample Business Plan Framework

Year (____) Real Estate Business Plan for

Especially prepared for

BUSINESS GOALS

Mission: Our mission is to create income by purchasing undervalued properties to remodel and sell or retain as long-term investments.

____________________ has over _____ years of experience as an investor and is *(Provide background on each investor's employment, real estate background, and other qualifications to invest in real estate.)*

Profit will be generated by:

(1) Performing cosmetic improvements to single-family homes and selling them to generate 40 to 50% profit

(2) Maintaining long-term rentals that generate a minimum of 10% cash on cash return

Short-Term Goals

We will create and uphold a reputation in our community for honesty in our business dealings, and we will aim to achieve win-win results. We will focus on acquiring distressed properties that can be fixed up and either sell them or use them as rentals.

During (year) we will purchase ___ properties to flip and ___ properties to rent. This will be the beginning of our long-term investment strategy to accumulate income-producing properties.

Actual number of properties purchased in (year):

flipped: ______ sold: _______ rentals: ______

Long-Term Goals

Our objective in (year) and each year until (year) will be to purchase an average of ___ properties per year to fix up and sell and ___ properties per year to increase our rental portfolio.

Pursuing this strategy over a five-year period will add ___ properties to our portfolio (single-family dwellings and duplexes) to go along with the ___ units currently in our portfolio (mix of single-family dwellings and multi-units, each returning an average of $_____ positive annual cash flow for a total annual income of $______ per year and annual asset appreciation of ___%.

Also, during this five-year period, it is our objective that more than ___ properties will be sold for an average of $____ profit each, for a total of more than $____ cash income.

Ownership

(Name of business)

We intend to be highly leveraged. All renovations will be done by licensed contractors.

DEVELOPING KNOWLEDGE OF THE MARKETPLACE

Target Neighborhoods

We will operate in the ______________________________ neighborhoods of the ____________________ metro area. This area was chosen because properties can be purchased in the price range of $_________ to $_________ and because of our significant knowledge of the area.

Selecting Properties

We have developed our strategy by purchasing properties in the $________ to $_______ price range. This price range represents the lower end of what properties are selling in the area, at least 20 to 40% less than average.

1. $______ between our purchase price and typical sales price is necessary to achieve our profit margin of approximately

____

2. For our rental portfolio, a purchase price of at least _____% price differential from market value is necessary for each purchase.

In order to appeal to homeowners and renters, these properties should be 3 bedrooms for resale and a minimum of 2 bedrooms for rentals. Properties should be located close to schools and shopping and should include amenities that will attract young families and first-time buyers.

Locating Flexible / Distressed Sellers

Our target market will be sellers who are highly motivated and may be having financial difficulties, or those whose properties have been on the market for at least _____ months.

Properties that initially will meet our criteria include:

1. Foreclosures
2. Properties in disrepair
3. Property management problems
4. Estate sales
5. Absentee ownership
6. Tenant problems
7. Retirement or relocation

It is anticipated that these sellers will be willing to negotiate to meet our minimum criteria for purchases.

Developing a Network

To be successful with our strategy, we will establish strong partnerships with real estate agents, banks, and others.

BUSINESS OPERATIONS

Target Customer

Age group: ____ to ____ years

1. Resale Properties

Our target buyer is a young, dual-income family. These buyers will have adequate to good credit but may lack significant cash reserves for a down payment or closing costs. Purchase price: $_______ to $________

Our approach to these buyers will be to utilize programs such as FHA, VA, and others.

2. Rentals

For our rental portfolio, our target market for tenants will include students, young couples, single parents, and dual-income families. The target rent will be $______ to $______ per month. These tenants will also serve as perfect candidates to purchase the property in the future.

Performing Market Analysis

The source we will use to determine the value of a property will be market analysis available through the Multiple Listing Service and our own experience over the past ___ years.

Financial Analysis

Each property to be purchased will be analyzed to determine the value of the property, appropriate purchase price, estimated cost of potential renovation, acquisition costs, and potential selling price as well as anticipated profit.

Financial Arrangements

We have established relationships with the following banks: so we will know in advance of our ability to purchase properties that meet our criteria.

As we will only purchase undervalued properties, after the renovations are completed, we will seek permanent financing based on appraisal.

Renovation Process

We intend to purchase properties that are sold well below market value and will require minimal cosmetic updates and improvements. We anticipate that every property will require at least some cosmetic improvements to increase its value. It is our intent for these properties to be sold within a 90- to 120-day period encompassing acquisition, remodeling, and purchase by buyer.

To perform these renovations as quickly and efficiently as possible, we have assembled an experienced crew that we have used extensively over the past ____ years. Additionally, we have enough experience and knowledge to determine the estimated costs and time frame required to complete each project. We anticipate that each project should be completed within 45 days from start to finish.

Based on our experience, the following improvements will significantly increase the value of each property:

1. Update kitchen: Install new cabinets if necessary, ceramic tile floor, new countertops, dishwasher, and other appliances.
2. Replace carpet, refinish wood floors, install new blinds.
3. Update bathroom fixtures including vanities.
4. Paint interior/exterior as necessary.
5. Perform landscaping to improve exterior appearance.
6. Perform general overall polishing of property. We will keep in mind that our target sale price is in the $100,000 to $120,000 range.

Each property will be evaluated on its own merits, but typical renovation costs are expected to range between $______ and $______. Properties that are purchased at $______ to $______ below market value will provide adequate profit to achieve our desired return within ____ to ____ days from acquisition.

Our renovation process model assumes that the six key tasks stated above represent the entire work to be completed. This assumption will be validated prior to purchase by means of a thorough inspection process. Our inspections will be done by contractors so there will be no surprises regarding the renovation costs.

On occasion, however, a property may be available that may require a much higher remodeling price that would be justified by an opportunity to make a lot more money. These properties may require structural improvements or other major remodeling. These could be properties that are in terrible disrepair.

Another exception to our typical purchase criteria may be a small property that is surrounded by much larger and more expensive homes in a very desirable neighborhood. These scenarios do not meet our investment strategy but may be considered depending on the money needed to complete the project.

Selling Properties

After each property has been renovated it will be listed for sale. As our target market consists of ____- to ___- year olds who may only have enough of a down payment for an FHA mortgage, we expect to help with closing costs.

Rental Portfolio

Careful attention will be given during the purchase process to find potential rental properties that would meet the criteria for our long-term investment portfolio. For these properties to meet our standards, they must pass the following performance measures:

1. We must be able to buy and fix up the property with minimal cash outlay.

2. The property must be in a desirable area (family-friendly neighborhood) to ensure better than average appreciation and better tenants, and it must be purchased at a price below market value.

3. The income and expense streams must be favorable to net a positive cash flow of at least $______ per year from each property.

Timeline

In summary, following the timeline identified throughout this document, we expect to purchase an average of ____ to ____ properties per month.

Managing Our Properties

We are a very successful enterprise with over _____ years of experience as investors. We have an excellent system in place to continue to monitor our portfolio. We know every month how each property is performing. This is accomplished by our monthly profit and loss statement. We are confident that our experience and success over the years merit strong consideration for approval of a working line of credit in the amount of $__________. Thank you very much for your consideration, and we look forward to establishing a mutually beneficial relationship.

____

How should investors take title to an investment property?

A very important decision that should be made as part of your business plan is how to take title to a property. How title is held has many consequences, and you should consult with an attorney to determine which of the many ownership options will be best for you. Keep in mind that some states have additional laws or restrictions regarding how one may hold title. The title company you use can be a tremendous resource for you.

The most common ways of taking title to an investment property are sole ownership, joint tenancy with right of survivorship, tenancy in common, revocable living trust, and establishment of a limited liability company.

Sole ownership

The simplest way to hold title is by sole ownership of the property. As the name implies, the sole owner holds all rights to the property. Although this form of ownership is mostly utilized by singles, theoretically speaking a married person can claim sole ownership of a property if his or her spouse is willing to sign a quit claim deed, which is a document that effectively denies the spouse any rights to the property. (Very few spouses are willing to do this.)

Joint tenancy with right of survivorship

Two or more people may hold title together in a form of ownership called joint tenancy. In this form of ownership, each owner has equal rights to the property. "Right of survivorship" means that if one owner dies, the deceased person's share will be automatically transferred to the co-owner(s) of the property rather than to the heirs of the deceased.

Tenancy in common

This structure is primarily used when there are partners involved. Under tenancy in common, multiple partners can hold either equal or unequal portions of the same property. For example, two people could each own 50% of the property, or they could split ownership 70% and 30%, or one person could own 50% and the other 50% could be split between 10 additional partners who each hold 5% ownership. Any combination of percentages is acceptable.

You may wonder what would keep one partner from independently selling his or her percentage without consulting the other partners. It is standard procedure to have a written agreement between the owners specifying how a partner can transfer his or her interest in the property.

Revocable living trust

In a living trust, title is held in the name of the trustee. Usually the person who establishes the trust serves as its trustee in order to keep full control of the property. The owner can buy, sell, and refinance just as if the property is not being held in the trust. One of the benefits of establishing a revocable trust is that if the person is no longer capable of performing the duties of trustee, the successor trustee (who was named when the trust was set up) will take over as trustee. For additional information on establishing a revocable trust, go to http://www.aarp.org/money/estate-planning.

Limited liability company (LLC)

Many investors choose to operate their real estate business as a limited liability company (better known as an LLC). Like a corporation, an LLC protects its members from liability. This means that members theoretically are not personally liable for debts incurred by the business. However, in my experience lenders will not loan money to an LLC unless the loan is also personally guaranteed by the members.

One of the major benefits of an LLC is that often court judgments incurred by the LLC do not affect the personal assets of the individual members. This protection is not provided by a sole proprietorship or traditional partnership.

Advantages of an LLC

1. Tax flexibility

The IRS does not consider an LLC to be a distinct, separate entity for tax purposes. This means that (at least initially) the IRS will not tax the LLC directly. Instead, members of the LLC get to determine how they want to be taxed. There are several options:

Single-member LLC: This structure is taxed like a sole proprietorship. Profits or losses from the business are not taxed directly but instead are taxed through the single member's personal tax return.

Partners in an LLC: Same as above, and profit and losses based on the percentage of ownership for tax purposes are taxed through the member's personal tax return.

Generally, members of an LLC will create an Articles of Organization and Operating Agreement that outlines how the LLC will be treated for tax purposes and so on. Further information on how the IRS classifies some LLCs can be found at http://www.irs.gov/

2. Less paperwork

Compared with C-Corps or S-Corps, LLCs are very flexible. With less stringent requirements for compliance and reduced paperwork, LLCs are easier to form and easier to keep in good legal standing. **(On a side note, if you want to find out more about the differences between an S Corp and a C Corp, go to** http://www.bizfilings.com.)

Disadvantages of an LLC

1. Self-employment taxes

Unless the LLC chooses to be taxed like a corporation, members of an LLC are usually subject to self-employment taxes. This means that the profits of the LLC won't be taxed at the corporate level but will pass through to its members who will account for those profits on their personal federal tax returns. Often these taxes are higher than they would be at the corporate level. Individual members will pay for their own Medicare and Social Security.

2. Confusion about roles

Corporations have specific roles (like directors, managers, and employees), but LLCs generally do not. This can make it hard to figure out who's in charge, who can sign certain contracts, and so on. This type of confusion can be avoided if roles of the members are outlined in the LLC's articles of organization and operating agreement.

3. Limited life

Corporations can live forever, whereas an LLC is dissolved when a member dies or undergoes bankruptcy.

In summary, LLCs provide a great degree of flexibility and protection to their members. They shield members from personal liability while providing many tax options.

The preceding information is intended only as a brief overview of the different ways of taking title to a property. Specific details should be discussed with an attorney or accountant.

Why do you need an exit plan?

In *The 7 Habits of Highly Effective People,* author Stephen R. Covey calls the second habit "Begin with the End in Mind." I could not think of more appropriate advice for real estate investors. What is the plan for each property? Why should investors start with the end in mind? Because every property should you purchase should bring you closer to one or more of your goals.

When I started investing more than 45 years ago, the idea of an exit strategy was the furthest thing from my mind. Now that I am in my late sixties it is time to ask "Now what? I'm not going to be around forever, so what should I do with my real estate portfolio?" The easiest answer is to hand it over to my kids. Unfortunately, I'm not sure whether I would be doing them a favor if I did that, because they might not have the same level of interest or commitment as I do.

At this point, you probably will agree that owning a worthwhile real estate portfolio is one of the better options for accomplishing financial prosperity. If your real estate business is successful, eventually you will have a sizable portfolio that provides substantial income and cash flow. Some investors will follow the exit strategy of "I'll hold onto my portfolio until I die," and depending on the size of the estate there may be significant tax consequences. Most of us, however, will choose different strategies that are more realistic and will sell some of our properties for one reason or another. Having an exit strategy is just as important as buying the property at a great price.

Why would an investor want to have an exit plan as they are rolling along in the accumulation mode? Simply stated, the answer is that the end can come sooner than expected.

When you purchase a property, you should ask yourself how long you intend to own it. Earlier in this chapter, we reviewed the definitions of A, B, C, or D properties and areas. With this information in mind, who would be the likely buyer when it's time to sell?

What about tax consequences? Unfortunately, Uncle Sam wants a piece of the action, so tax planning is critical. This is probably the most important strategy of all because we only want to pay our fair share of taxes.

Possible exits

There are several different ways to sell a real estate investment and collect your profits. These may include the following:

1. *Wholesale:* Buy the property and sell it quickly to another investor.

2. *Sell/Flip:* Buy the property, improve it, and sell it to someone who wants to live in it (owner-occupied property).

3. *Rental:* Use the property as a long-term rental and then sell it.

4. *Lease option:* Lease it with the idea that in a year or two the renter may be able to buy. Perhaps they have good income but poor credit and in time they may be able to improve their credit score. With a lease option, tenants accept responsibility for repairs and maintenance. As a result, they tend to take their rental obligation seriously.

5. Seller financing: If the owner has the property paid in full, seller financing for the right buyer may be a good option. This strategy alleviates paying capital gains all at once. Seek the advice of a CPA to see if this option makes sense for you.

6. *1031 tax exchange:* Thanks to IRC Section 1031, a properly structured 1031 exchange allows an investor to sell a property, reinvest the proceeds in a new property, and defer all capital gain taxes. This is probably the best exit strategy from a tax standpoint.

7. *Charitable giving:* Charitable giving is always an option. There are many methods of contributing, so it is best to seek the advice of an attorney or CPA.

Many real estate investors have spent a lot of time and energy building their portfolios but have paid very little time attention to designing their exit strategy. Having a plan now will help you make better decisions for the future. A good exit strategy takes account of personal goals for income, family, retirement, lifestyle, wealth preservation, income tax, and estate planning.

It is imperative to have a competent attorney or CPA on your team to assist you in making these decisions.

Key points to remember:

- ✓ Real estate investing should be treated as a business.
- ✓ Writing a business plan helps you chart your progress toward short- and long-term goals and also makes it easier to borrow money from banks.
- ✓ How a business is owned and operated affects taxation and estate planning.
- ✓ As with any other business, real estate investors should have an exit strategy.

Chapter 14

LEVERAGING A 1031 EXCHANGE, SELF-FUNDING, AND ROTH IRA

Details on the 1031 exchange

For real estate investors, the 1031 exchange is one of the most powerful tools for managing tax liability when selling and purchasing investment properties.

Normally, when property is sold, any gain on the sale will be taxed. However, the 1031 exchange allows you to defer capital gains tax on the sale of an investment property if you use the proceeds to purchase any type of real estate. This tax deferral provides you with more capital to invest in a subsequent purchase.

To understand the advantages a 1031 exchange offers, consider the following example:

> An investor has a $200,000 capital gain and incurs a tax liability of approximately $70,000 in combined taxes (depreciation recapture, federal and state capital gain taxes) when a property is sold. Only $130,000 remains to reinvest in another property. Assuming a 25% down payment and a 75% loan-to-value ratio, the seller would be able to purchase properties worth $520,000.
>
> If the same investor chooses a 1031 exchange, however, he or she can reinvest the entire $200,000 of equity in the purchase of $800,000 in real estate, assuming the same down payment and loan-to-value ratios.

Anyone contemplating using a 1031 exchange to purchase real estate should seek the advice of a competent attorney or CPA.

Using self-directed or Roth IRAs to buy real estate

Want to have more control over your financial future? Consider using a self-directed or Roth IRA to purchase real estate.

Many investors and real estate agents are unaware that retirement funds such as self-directed and Roth IRAs can be utilized to invest in real estate such as rentals for long-term income or properties to fix and flip for quicker profits. Investors can even benefit from real estate without owning the property itself by using IRA funds to purchase mortgage notes and trust deeds secured by real estate.

A real estate IRA is technically no different from any other IRA (or 401k). The government created the IRA to allow investments to grow tax-free or tax-deferred with the proceeds compounded over time to maximize growth. The IRA provides asset protection so that assets can be passed down to future generations.

What kinds of real estate can be purchased using an IRA?

With an IRA, an investor has the freedom to invest in almost any form of real estate, including the following:

- Homes, apartments, and condominiums
- Commercial properties such as retail stores, hotels, and office complexes
- Trust deed notes, mortgages, and tax liens
- Undeveloped land, lots, and farmland

Key differences between purchasing real estate with an IRA and making a traditional investment

Purchasing and maintaining real estate in a retirement account differs from traditional property investments in a few important ways:

- The property's buyer is the IRA, not the investor. That's why paperwork must flow through an IRA custodian like Pensco, New Direction IRA Inc., Equity Trust, Broad Financial, or others. I am mostly familiar with Pensco because a couple of my clients use their services.

- All expenses and revenue must go through the IRA. Expenses must be paid by the IRA, and any revenue must come into the IRA.

- The investor cannot use the property for personal reasons. The property must be treated as investment, not used for the immediate benefit of you, your business, or your family.

- Maintenance and repairs must be done by a third party. If the IRA owner provides any "sweat equity" activities — even something as minor as changing a light bulb — there could be significant tax penalties.

What is a self-directed IRA?

A self-directed IRA allows the account owner to direct the account trustee to make a broader range of investments than other types of IRAs.

Internal Revenue Service (IRS) regulations require that either a qualified trustee or custodian hold the IRA assets on behalf of the IRA owner. Generally, the trustee/custodian will maintain the assets and all transactions and other records pertaining to them, file required IRS reports, issue client statements, help clients understand the rules regarding prohibited transactions, and perform other administrative duties on behalf of the self-directed IRA owner for the life of the IRA account. The custodian of a self-directed IRA may offer a selection of standard asset types that the account owner can invest in, such as stocks, bonds, and mutual funds, but the account owner also can make other types of investments, such as real estate. The range of permissible investments is broad but regulated by the IRS. The major benefit is that gains will not be taxed until they are distributed during retirement.

What is a Roth IRA?

A Roth IRA is a self-directed retirement account that is funded with post-tax dollars. Although contributions are not tax-deductible, the tax benefit of a Roth IRA is that all earnings, including interest, capital gains, and dividend income, grow tax-free. Income taxes are paid on initial contributions in the year they are made, but the account holder can withdraw the earnings tax-free if certain requirements are met.

In addition, direct contributions can be withdrawn at any time without penalty because these funds have already been taxed. Account holders can begin withdrawing earnings at age

59½ but are not required to take distributions at any age.

A Roth IRA gives the account holder the freedom to invest in almost any form of real estate. The key benefit is that it is all tax-free and you can grow it as much as you want.

Anyone who is contemplating using their IRA to purchase real estate should seek the advice of a competent CPA and attorney and consult with the appropriate custodians.

Key points to remember:

- ✓ Using a 1031 exchange defers taxation of capital gains and gives you greater purchasing power.
- ✓ You can purchase real estate using funds from a self-directed or Roth IRA, and this type of financing brings both advantages and disadvantages.

Chapter 15

PUTTING IT ALL TOGETHER

I decided to write this book because I wanted to share the strategies and systems that have worked well for me during my forty-five years as an investor and for the past twenty years as a real estate agent. The financial benefits of investing in real estate have been substantial for me, but the money I've made has not been the only reward. My life has also been enriched through longtime friendships with many of my former clients, tenants, and colleagues.

If you have been sitting on the sidelines while others are reaping the financial benefits of real estate investing, I hope reading this book has helped you decide to get in the "game." You now have knowledge and hopefully, the confidence to make your real estate investment business very lucrative for you and your family.

Put your newfound knowledge to use

You are now able to do more than just talk about investing. You have enough knowledge to take the necessary steps. Remember wealth is found on the other side of fear.

- You should know your short- and long-term objectives.
- You are now equipped with the information to make good business decisions.

- You can identify properties that have investment potential.
- You can analyze whether a property is likely to be a poor, good, or great investment. (Remember that price alone doesn't determine whether a property is a good deal.)
- You should be able to connect with contractors, property management companies, bankers, accountants, attorneys, and people in the trades.

Now that you are armed with this knowledge, the sky is the limit and you must decide how far you want to go in your real estate investment business. Your strategy can include a mix of buy-and-hold or flip, and both options can let you enjoy the financially security you deserve in years to come.

Although great deals are no longer as readily available as they were in the past, you will succeed if you clearly describe your target properties and neighborhoods in your overall business plan and goals.

You now understand the different strategies for buy-and-hold versus buy-and-flip. Additionally, you are familiar with some of the tax benefits available to you. You should always seek the advice of a competent accountant so that you will pay no more than your fair share of taxes.

An action plan for success

Believe in yourself. Know that you can generate wealth and retirement income, perhaps much more than you have achieved so far with your other investments or with your financial advisor. It is my view that you know much better what your financial needs are than anyone else could. I am sure you will agree with me that being in control of your own financial future is much better than having someone else control it. Remember that real estate is one of the better vehicles for wealth building and one of the few options that can provide tax benefits.

One mistake I have seen often is that many investors think they can do this on their own. In my opinion, working with the right real estate agent can be the quickest path to help you accomplish your financial objectives. I would strongly encourage you to be extremely loyal and to expect the same degree of commitment from your agent. You are looking to build wealth, and since agents are independent contractors, they have a vested interest in finding properties that meet your needs so that they can earn a commission. Your relationship with your real estate agent is a classic example of a WIN-WIN partnership.

As you know, the real estate industry is filled with get-rich-quick programs from so called "gurus" who make big promises but never deliver. Instead of paying thousands of dollars to purchase systems or attend a seminar, use the money as part of a down payment or for repairs.

The most important person that you should think of is the real estate agent you decide to use. Never underestimate the influence your agent can have as your coach, mentor, and advisor. They won't charge a dime for their services when representing you as a buyer's agent. Who knows more about your community—your agent or someone who comes to town for a one-night-stand and leaves the next day?

Your real estate agent can look on the MLS to find properties and open doors. They should be able to analyze a property and tell you if it is a good deal or if you should walk away from it because it will not meet your objectives. They can help you run the numbers to ensure that aren't leaving things up to chance. They can tell you about properties that are not even listed if they don't have a buyer. Always keep in mind that when you achieve your goals, your agent will also achieve theirs.

Knowledge is powerful, and you now have enough expertise to succeed and grow your business.

The actions you take during the next 30 days could change your life. (You can use the "30-day Action Plan Worksheet" in the Resources section to get started.)

You are well on your way to building wealth with real estate, and I wish you much success. If I can do it, so can you. Congratulations! Drop me an email at reinvestorsclientsforlife@gmail.com or call me at 402-679-3914 to ask questions or offer suggestions for the next edition of this book. Your feedback would be greatly appreciated!

RESOURCES

Purchasing this book entitles you to download the documents in this section at no additional charge.

To download, go to
www.realestateclientsforlife.com

An open letter to tenants who don't pay the rent on time

What would you do if you worked hard all week long and on payday your boss told you that you were not going to get paid and ... that you would have to wait and wait and wait for your money and... that he did not know when (or if) you would ever get paid?

How long would you work without getting paid? How would you feel? And what would you do about it? Would you just say, "Okay, I understand. Just pay me whenever you can?" Or would you...

Call your boss on the phone? What if he refused to return your calls? Would you send letters? What if your letters were ignored? Then what would you do? Would you go to his or her office? Would you argue? Would you report your boss to a government agency whose job is to protect working people like you? Would you hire a lawyer and pay big bucks that you will never see again? Would you agree to pay court costs and the legal fees that begin to pile up the moment you tell you lawyer to sue? The bottom line is you would not be very happy as your bills would pile up and then you would have to borrow money from relatives, friends, etc., to pay your bills, buy groceries, put gas in your car, and on and on. You likely would have to make choices as to what bills you would pay first, right? For sure you would buy groceries, gas to get to work, pay your utilities, etc., and other bills, and maybe if anything was left over you would pay part of the rent, and I wonder why.

Unfortunately, as a property owner I don't have many choices with the bank as my mortgage payment must be paid on time each and every month; otherwise, I am charged a late-payment penalty and my credit score is affected. The bank doesn't care if you pay your rent on time or not, but I do. If you don't, I'll get into financial difficulties myself. I have to make choices of which bills I pay first, and the answer is always my mortgage before anything else, and in your case it should be your rent.

So in conclusion, I expect to receive the rent on time each and every month, just as you expect to get your paycheck on time each and every time. My guess is that you would not be very happy if you did not get your paycheck on time, so hopefully the next time you are thinking about picking up the phone, or I have to call you and you tell me that you cannot pay your rent on time this month because (fill in the blank), it will not make me very happy either, so I hope you understand.

Someone gave me this list of reasons why the rent is late. Hopefully, none of these will apply to your situation.

I'm sorry my rent is late, but…

___ A. **The check I've been waiting for did not come in the mail.**

___ B. **I was in the hospital/jail and I couldn't get to you.**

___ C. **I missed a week of work because I had to take care of my sick mother / son / daughter.**

___ D. **I had to have some teeth pulled and the dentist won't start work until I give him some money.**

___ E. **I was in an automobile accident and I won't have any money until my attorney works things out with the other guy's insurance.**

___ F. I had my billfold stolen when this guy jumped me on my way to the bank / post office / my office.

___ G. Someone broke into my place and took my money. No, I didn't file a police report. Should I?

___ H. I had to have my car fixed so I could get to work, so I could pay you.

___ I. My mother / sister / uncle hasn't mailed me my money yet.

___ J. I couldn't find your address, and I put the wrong address on the envelope.

___ K. I got laid off from my job and I won't get unemployment for a couple of weeks.

___ L. I was not able to get a money order and I know you didn't want me to send cash.

___ M. You didn't come by when I had the money.

___ N. My husband / wife / boyfriend / girlfriend / roommate left and I didn't have all the money.

___ O. They garnished my check and I don't understand it, because the guy told me it would be okay to just pay so much per month and I only missed a couple of payments.

___ P. I told my friend to bring it or send it to you while I was out of town.

___ Q. I haven't received my tax refund yet.

___ R. I got a new job, and I have to work three weeks before I get my first check.

___ S. I didn't pay the rent because my ___ is not fixed. No, I'm sorry I didn't tell you there was a problem before now. I didn't think about it until now.

___ T. My car is broken and I didn't have a ride to your office.

___ U. I had to help my brother / sister / friend who had a serious problem.

___ V. **I didn't have, or I forgot to put, a stamp on the envelope.**
___ W. **The check is in the mail. Didn't you get it?**
___ X. **I ran out of checks.**

Please briefly explain if you reason is not listed above.

____
____
____
____
____

You will never get penalized for paying your rent early; however, you will pay a late payment penalty of $25 if the rent is not paid in full by midnight on the third day after the rent is due, plus an additional $5 per day until the rent is paid in full.

Tax deductions for real estate investors

[Note: Keep in mind that tax rules involving real estate are complicated. For example, an investor who owns multiple rental properties will need to file a special form with the IRS if they want to treat all their real estate interests as a single activity for tax purposes. If they don't do this, each rental property will count as a separate business. Anyone who is thinking about investing in real estate should seek the advice of a qualified tax attorney or accountant.]

As a real estate investor, you will benefit from a number of tax deductions. One of the most substantial deductions is for depreciation, described in more detail below. In addition to depreciation, the following expenses also are deductible:

- *Home office.* Anyone who works from home can take the home office deduction. This means that a portion of the expenses you pay for your primary residence, such as mortgage payments, tax and insurance, utility payments, and so on, can be deducted as home office expenses.

- *Office supplies, cell phone for business, and so on.* Just about anything purchased for the office may be deductible if it is used for your real estate business.

- *Business expenses* – You can deduct the cost of subscriptions, dues, and fees for membership in real estate organizations such as property owners' or investors' groups as well as expenses for attending real estate conventions.

- *Mileage* – You can deduct mileage if your personal vehicle is used for business purposes.

- *Real estate professional* – For tax purposes, anyone (not just a full-time real estate agent) can be considered a "real estate professional" if they spend at least 750 hours per year involved in real property trades and businesses *and* if more than half (at least 51%) of the personal services they perform during the year involve real property trades and businesses. One of the biggest benefits of investing in real estate is the ability to offset real estate paper losses (primarily caused by depreciation) against other income. If you meet the IRS criteria to qualify as a real estate professional, then 100% of your paper real estate losses may be used to offset your other income, reducing the amount you owe the government. Even if you do *not* qualify as a real estate professional for IRS purposes, you can deduct up to $25,000 of your rental real estate losses from your other income if you actively participate in your real estate business.
- Taxes and insurance on the property are deductible.
- Expenses for repairs and upkeep are deductible.
- Fees paid to a property management company and to your attorney and accountant are deductible. (By the way, you should find an accountant who is knowledgeable about tax laws related to real estate investment. My guess is that if you had your tax returns prepared by 100 accountants you would get 100 different tax returns.)

How is depreciation calculated for income tax purposes?

After determining the cost or another tax basis for the rental property, you must allocate the basis amount among the various types of property you're renting. When we speak of types of property, we refer to certain components of your rental, such as the land, the building itself, and personal property such as the stove, refrigerator, and dishwasher you provide with the rental, and so on. Why this effort to divide your tax basis between property types? Because each type is depreciated using different rules.

Below are the most common divisions of tax basis for a rental property, followed by explanations of the different methods of depreciation that generally apply:

Type of Property	*Method of Depreciation*	*Useful Life in Years*
Land	Not allowed	N/A
Residential rental real estate	Straight line	27.5
Commercial real estate	Straight line	39
Shrubbery, fences, driveways, etc.	150% declining balance	15
Appliances, etc.	200% declining balance	5

In *straight-line depreciation*, the cost basis is spread evenly over the tax life of the property. For example, a residential rental building with a cost basis of $120,000 would generate depreciation of $4,363 per year ($120,000 /2 7.5 years). (This does not include personal property, land improvement or land, only the actual property.)

In the year that the rental is first placed in service (rented), your deduction is prorated based on the number of months that the property is rented or held out for rent, with 1/2 month for the first month. If the building in the example above is placed in service in August, you can take a deduction for 4½ months' worth of depreciation, amounting to $1,636.12 (4.5 X $4,363/12).

Recovery percentages for five-year personal property: This kind of depreciation is calculated by multiplying the rate of the straight-line depreciation by the adjusted balance of the property at the start of each year over the remaining life of the property. To make matters somewhat easier, the IRS and others publish tables of percentages that can be applied to the original cost to determine yearly depreciation. For instance, below are annual depreciations for personal property with the 200% declining balance:

Year	**Percentage**
1	20.00
2	32.00
3	19.20
4	11.52
5	11.52
6	5.76
Total	100%

Examples: The 200% declining balance depreciation on $2,000 worth of appliances used in a rental would be $384 in Year 3 ($2,000 X .192).

Examples of personal property that can be depreciated over five years might include a snow blower, lawn mower, carpet, furniture, computer, and so on.

Examples of land improvements that can be depreciated over 15 years are sidewalks, fences, landscaping, and shrubbery.

30 DAY ACTION PLAN WORKSHEET

Name:

MY ANNUAL GOAL

YEAR ________

MY MONTHLY GOAL

MONTH OF________

MY ONE MONTH GOAL

WEEK 1	WEEK 2	WEEK 3	WEEK 4

Property Checklist

Print out a few copies of this checklist to use as you visit prospective properties. Having information on each property can help you to compare properties and will make your final decision much easier.

Date ______________________________
Address ___________________________ Price _____________
Property taxes _______________
How long has it been on the market? _____ Foreclosure _____yes _____no
Other____
____

Age of property _______ Neighborhood/Subdivision ________________
Corner lot __ yes __no
Overall impression of Area/Neighborhood __Acceptable __ Not acceptable
Overall impression of properties on either side and /across from subject property
__Acceptable __ Not acceptable
Other____
____

Style
__ 2.5 Story __ 2 Story__1.5 Story __Bungalow __Multi level __ Ranch
__ Split entry __ Raised ranch
__ Tri level __ Cape Cod __ Townhouse __ Condo __Other

Type of Construction
__ Wood __ Brick __Stone __ Stucco __ Vinyl siding __ Aluminum siding __ Other

Exterior Features
Roof type __________
Roof condition ___ Good ___ Fair ___ Acceptable __ Needs replaced
Fenced ___yes ___no Porch ___yes ___no Deck __yes ___no
Patio __yes __no Deck __yes ___no
Other____
Paint ___ Acceptable ___ Needs painted
Other____
____

Garage
___ 1 car __ 2 car __Attached __Detached __ Carport
___ no garage __off-street parking

Central AC __ yes __no Window units __yes __no # of units _____________

Interior Features

Kitchen
Eat-In __yes__no_____Size __________
Type of flooring __Ceramic tile __Wood floors__ Linoleum __Other _______
Appliances __ yes __no Stove__yes __ ___ no
Refrigerator __yes __ no Dishwasher __yes __ no Other ________
Condition of cabinets ___ new___old ___ Painted: yes __no ____
Needs replacing __yes __no

Dining Room
___yes ___no Size ____________ Carpet yes___no___ Wood floors yes___no___

Living Room
Size ____________ Carpet ___yes __ no Wood floors yes __no
Other____

Den/Family room Size ____________
Carpet __yes __no Wood floors___yes __ no

Other rooms____

Total bedrooms___________

Bedroom 1 size ____________ Carpet __yes __no Wood floors yes __ no
Other ____________________

Bedroom 2 size ____________ Carpet __yes __no Wood floors yes __ no
Other ____________________

Bedroom 3 size ____________ Carpet __yes __no Wood floors yes __ no
Other ____________________

Bedroom 4 size ____________ Carpet __yes __no Wood floors yes __ no
Other ____________________

____
____

Total bathrooms __________
Full____ 3/4____ 1/2_____ 1/4 ____
Master bath ___ yes ___ no Flooring type________________________________
Guest/powder bath ___ yes ___ no Flooring type___________________________
Other____

Laundry room
Location _______________ Washer ___yes ___no Dryer ___yes ___no
Other ____

Basement ___yes ___no Finished ___yes ___no _____
Flooring Carpet ____________Tile ____________ Other ____________

Utilities
Type of Heating
_____Gas_____Steam ___Hot water _____Electric _____ Oil
Age of System ________

Age/Capacity of water heater________ Gas_____ Electric_____

Electrical service
____Fuses ____Circuit breakers

Plumbing
Galvanized _____Copper _____Other _____________________________________
Sump pump/Drainage system: ___yes ___no
Sewer connected to public sewer ___yes ___no Septic ____yes ____no
Other____

Proximity to:
____ Schools____ Shopping ____Highways ____Religious institutions
____Downtown ____ Hospitals
Other____
____
____

Other things of interest nearby:
____
____
____
____

Recent sales of comparable properties in neighborhood

Address ______________________________ Sq. Ft __________
Price __________
# of bedrooms ____ # of baths____
Other features____
____

Address ______________________________ Sq. Ft __________
Price __________
# of bedrooms ____ # of baths____
Other features____
____

Address ______________________________ Sq. Ft __________
Price __________
# of bedrooms ____ # of baths____
Other features____
____

Notes

____
____
____
____
____
____
____
____
____
____
____
____
____
____
____
____
____
____
____

Multi-unit due diligence checklist

Due diligence involves much more than doing an actual property inspection with an inspector. Inspections are important, but they are only a tiny part of the process. Leaving no stones unturned will go a long way toward uncovering most potential problems.

When you are considering the purchase of a multi-unit, it is critically important to gather as much information as possible. The financial details are especially important, because you will need to use them when you run the numbers to see whether the property is a good investment.

In summary, the physical and financial due diligence process will uncover critical information that will help you decide to either move forward or to back out of the deal. Carrying out due diligence can save you from making a costly mistake.

Property details
Property address:
____
Asking price: $________________________
Type of property: A__ B__C__ D__
Legal description:
____
Parcel no. _______________________
Tax assessed value (year) ____________
Land value _________________________
Bldg. value _________________________
Existing financing (if any):
Lender (1st): _________________ (2nd):____________
Interest rate: _______
Term of loan: # of years ____
# of years remaining on loan ____
Is property being managed property management company?
________________________ by a _______
Contact: ____________________________
% charged monthly: _______

Financial details
It is important to obtain as much of the following financial information as possible.

- Profit and loss statements (P&L) for past 2-3 years [ ] Yes [ ] No

  Any concerns noted:

____

____

____

- Year to date income and expense statement [ ] Yes [ ] No
  Any concerns noted:
  ____
  ____
  ____

- Tax returns for past 2 to 3 years [ ] Yes [ ] No

  Any concerns noted:
  ____
  ____
  ____

- Secure and review rent rolls for past 2-3 years [ ] Yes [ ] No

  Any concerns noted:
  ____
  ____
  ____

- Secure copies of all leases [ ] Yes [ ] No

  Any concerns noted:
  ____
  ____
  ____

- Number of units that will become vacant in the next 3 months ___

  6 months___ 9 months___

  Any concerns noted:
  ____
  ____
  ____

- Secure copies of any service agreements (i.e., washer and dryer , security system, cable, other)? [ ] Yes [ ] No
  If yes, do any of them commit new buyer to be assumed?
  [ ] Yes [ ] No

- Does seller own washers / dryers? [ ] Yes [ ] No
- Any snow removal/ lawn mowing contracts? [ ] Yes [ ] No
- Secure copies of any major improvements/updates for past 2-3 years? [ ] Yes [ ] No
- Any concerns noted:

  ____

  ____

  ____

- Secure list of personal property to be included in the sale? [ ] Yes [ ] No

  ____

  ____

  ____

  ____

  ____

  ____

  ____

  ____

- Secure report of most recent accounts receivable? [ ] Yes [ ] No
- Secure report of delinquent rents/possible evictions? [ ] Yes [ ] No
- Are there any tenants with concessions (reduced rent, free rent, etc.)? [ ] Yes [ ] No If yes, how many of tenants fall in this category? __________
- Secure current listing of vendors, contractors handyman, electrician, plumber, other? [ ] Yes [ ] No

  ____

  ____

  ____

  ____

- Pet policy and rules: .Are pets allowed? [ ] Yes [ ] No
  If yes, how many units have pets? _____

Other details

- Any known code violations? [ ] Yes [ ] No
- Any environmental concerns? [ ] Yes [ ] No
  Mold: [ ] Yes [ ] No
  Lead paint: [ ] Yes [ ] No
  Asbestos: [ ] Yes [ ] No
  Any other concerns noted:

____
____
____

Insurance

- Secure a copy of current insurance policy and agent to compare / verify that you can obtain a satisfactory insurance quote?
  [ ] Yes [ ] No

Interior inspection

- Number of units__ How many: Efficiency __ 1 bedroom ___
  2 bedrooms ____ 3 bedrooms
- Checked interior of all units? [ ] Yes [ ] No
- Overall condition of units: Excellent ___ Good___ Poor___
  Needs lots of attention____
  Any repairs that will require immediate attention:
  ____
  ____
  ____
  ____
- Any vacant units noticed? [ ] Yes [ ] No If yes, which ones?
  ____
  ____
  ____
- Any repairs to units that will require immediate attention? Which units?
  ____
  ____
  ____
  ____
  ____
  ____
  ____
- Any pest/rodent/ problems noticed? [ ] Yes [ ] No
- Condition of appliances: Excellent ___ Good ___ Poor ___
  Appliances that need to be replaced:
  ____
  ____
  ____
  ____

- Any water/fire damage noted? [ ] Yes [ ] No If yes, which unit(s)?____
- Any problem tenants noticed? [ ] Yes [ ] No
- Security system? [ ] Yes [ ] No

Basement

- Are units separately metered for gas? [ ] Yes [ ] No
- Are units separately metered for electricity? [ ] Yes [ ] No
- Service panel fuses? [ ] Yes [ ] No
- Service panel circuit breakers? [ ] Yes [ ] No
- Is heating system boiler? [ ] Yes [ ] No
- If no, how many furnaces? ______ Age if known_____
- Number of water heaters_______ Age if known_______.
  Any recent updates?

Exterior details

- Condition of roof (age if known ________) Excellent ___ Good___ Poor___ Needs to be replaced [ ] Yes [ ] No
- Condition of windows and doors: Old or new? ____ Excellent ____ Good___ Poor___ Need to be replaced______________________
  Anything else of concern:
- Condition of soffits and fascia: Excellent ___ Good___ Poor___ Needs work______
- Condition of paint: Excellent ___ Good___ Poor___ Needs repainting_____
- Condition of gutters and downspouts: Excellent ___ Good___ Poor___ Needs to be replaced____
- Condition of chimney: Excellent ___ Good___ Poor___ Needs repair ___

- Condition of yard: Excellent ___ Good___ Needs lots of attention____

  ____

  ____

  ____
- Parking situation: Is it on street parking? [ ] Yes [ ] No
- If off street, for how many spots? ____
- Overall condition of exterior: Excellent ___ Good___ Poor___
  Any potential issues? [ ] Yes [ ] No

Area

- Overall impression of area: Excellent ___ Good____ Poor___
  Area/neighborhood rating: A__B__C__D___
- Anything else positive or negative that could cause you to walk away or move forward?

  ____

  ____
- How many apartments within a two-block area? ______________
- Overall conditions and general appearance of the area within a two-block area of the property under consideration:

  ____

  ____
- Any recent updates to exterior? [ ] Yes [ ] No
  If yes, describe:

  ____

  ____

  ____

  ____
- Any trends and changes in the area that could have a positive or negative influence in the future (i.e., new condos, apartments, offices, commercial buildings, etc.)? [ ] Yes [ ] No
  If yes, describe:

  ____

  ____

  How many new buildings are being constructed in the area? ______
- Other observations:

  ____

____

____

Inspections

- Any structural inspections needed? [ ] Yes [ ] No
  If yes, what type?

  ____

  ____

  ____

  ____

- Any contractor inspections needed? [ ] Yes [ ] No
  If yes, what type?

  ____

  ____

  ____

  ____

- Any mechanical inspection needed? [ ] Yes [ ] No
  If yes, what type?

  ____

  ____

  ____

  ____

Remodeling Cost Estimator

Property Address ______________________________ **Date** ____________________

Remodeling to be completed

Kitchen	**Item**	**Cost**	**Subtotal**
1.	______________________________	________	________
2.	______________________________	________	________
3.	______________________________	________	________
4.	______________________________	________	________
5.	______________________________	________	________
6.	______________________________	________	________
7.	______________________________	________	________
8.	______________________________	________	________

Bathroom	**Item**	**Cost**	**Subtotal**
1.	______________________________	________	________
2.	______________________________	________	________
3.	______________________________	________	________
4.	______________________________	________	________
5.	______________________________	________	________

Living Room	**Item**	**Cost**	**Subtotal**
1.	______________________________	________	________
2.	______________________________	________	________
3.	______________________________	________	________
4.	______________________________	________	________
5.	______________________________	________	________

Dining Room	Item	Cost	Subtotal
1.	____________	______	______
2.	____________	______	______
3.	____________	______	______
4.	____________	______	______
5.	____________	______	______

Bedroom 1	Item	Cost	Subtotal
1.	____________	______	______
2.	____________	______	______
3.	____________	______	______
4.	____________	______	______

Bedroom 2	Item	Cost	Subtotal
1.	____________	______	______
2.	____________	______	______
3.	____________	______	______
4.	____________	______	______

Bedroom 3	Item	Cost	Subtotal
1.	____________	______	______
2.	____________	______	______
3.	____________	______	______
4.	____________	______	______

Basement	Item	Cost	Subtotal
1.	________________	______	______
2.	________________	______	______
3.	________________	______	______
4.	________________	______	______

Exterior	Item	Cost	Subtotal
1.	________________	______	______
2.	________________	______	______
3.	________________	______	______
4.	________________	______	______

Misc.	Item	Cost	Subtotal
1.	________________	______	______
2.	________________	______	______
3.	________________	______	______
4.	________________	______	______
5.	________________	______	______

Total ________

Make-Ready Checklist

Property Address:________________________________

1. Make sure stove, refrigerator, and dishwasher are clean.
2. Make sure kitchen cabinets are clean and open and close properly.
3. Clean bathroom medicine cabinet, clean and caulk shower/tub, clean toilet and make sure seat is secured.
4. Make sure all windows open and close, have locks, and are clean.
5. Make sure there are no broken and/or missing blinds and all work properly.
6. Check furnace filter and change if necessary.
7. Make sure garage is clean.
8. Make sure all doors open and close properly and storm doors have closers and chains.
9. Make sure there are no broken screens or broken glass on storm windows and doors.
10. Check entire yard to make sure there's no junk and grass is cut.
11. Check all electrical outlets to make sure all work.
12. Make sure there are no burned out lightbulbs.

13. Make sure smoke and carbon monoxide detectors are working.
14. Make sure there is one carbon monoxide detector on each finished floor.
15. Make sure there is one smoke detector in each bedroom, one in basement, and one between the living room and kitchen.
16. Check all closets to make sure they are clean and have closet rods.
17. Check all ceiling fans to make sure they work and are clean.
18. Make sure there are no leaks under kitchen and bathroom sinks and faucets are working properly.
19. Check/wipe all walls to make sure they are clean, and touch up with paint as necessary.
20. Check for mold in basement and under sinks in kitchen and bathroom, and clean with mold spray as needed.
21. Make sure entire house has been cleaned.
22. Make sure yard is mowed and any yard waste has been removed.
23. Make sure gutters are clean.
24. Make sure there are no missing corners on siding.
25. Make sure all drains work properly.
26. Make sure all interior/exterior handrails are secured.
27. Make sure carpet is clean

Notes

Date completed:____________________________________

Signature:____

Real Estate Rehab worksheet

Address

PURCHASE COSTS	
Loan Origination	$ 1,000.00
Appraisal	$ 400.00
Credit Report	$ 70.00
Title Insurance	$ 425.00
Escrow Fee	$ 175.00
Recording Fee	$ 50.00
Other	
TOTAL PURCHASE COSTS	**$ 2,120.00**
RENOVATION COSTS	
Holding Costs	
Interest	$ 3,600.00
Property Taxes	$ 600.00
Insurance	$ 150.00
Utilities	
Gas, Water, Sewer, Electrical	$ 350.00
Trash service	$ 75.00
Other	
SUBTOTAL HOLDING COSTS	**$ 4,775.00**
FIX-UP COSTS	
Clean up/Demolition	$ 350.00
Electrical	$ 500.00
Plumbing	$ 500.00
Painting/drywall	$ 1,000.00
Kitchen Remodel	
Bathroom Remodel	
Flooring	$ 800.00
Carpet	$ 2,500.00

	Good	Better	Best
PURCHASE PRICE	$ 85,000.00	$ 80,000.00	$ 75,000.00
RENOVATION COSTS	$ 2,120.00	$ 2,120.00	$ 2,120.00
HOLDING COSTS	$ 4,775.00	$ 4,775.00	$ 4,775.00
FIXUP COSTS	$ 6,150.00	$ 6,150.00	$ 6,150.00
	$ 98,045.00	$ 93,045.00	$ 88,045.00

PROPOSED SALES PRICE	$ 120,000.00	$ 125,000.00	$ 130,000.00
LESS SALES COSTS	$ 6,000.00	$ 7,000.00	$ 8,000.00
Title Insurance	$ 500.00	$ 500.00	$ 500.00
Document Stamps	$ 300.00	$ 300.00	$ 300.00
Other			
Other			
Other			
Net Proceeds To Seller	$ 113,200.00	$ 117,200.00	$ 121,200.00
Total Profit / Loss	$ 15,155.00	$ 24,155.00	$ 33,155.00

NOTES:

Real Estate Rehab worksheet

Address

PURCHASE COSTS	
Loan Origination	$
Appraisal	$
Credit Report	$
Title Insurance	$
Escrow Fee	$
Recording Fee	$
Other	
TOTAL PURCHASE COSTS	**$**
RENOVATION COSTS	
Holding Costs	
Interest	$
Property Taxes	$
Insurance	$
Utilities	
Gas, Water, Sewer, Electrical	$
Trash service	$
Other	
SUBTOTAL HOLDING COSTS	**$**
FIX-UP COSTS	
Clean up/Demolition	$
Electrical	$
Plumbing	$
Painting/drywall	$
Kitchen Remodel	
Bathroom Remodel	
Flooring	$
Carpet	$
Roof, Siding, Windows	
Landscape/Lawn	$
Other	
SUBTOTAL FIX UP COSTS	**$**
TOTAL COSTS	**$**

	Good	Better	Best
PURCHASE PRICE	$	$	$
RENOVATION COSTS	$	$	$
HOLDING COSTS	$	$	$
FIXUP COSTS	$	$	$
	$	$	$

PROPOSED SALES PRICE	$	$	$
LESS SALES COSTS	$	$	$
Title Insurance	$	$	$
Document Stamps	$	$	$
Other			
Other			
Other			
Net Proceeds To Seller	$	$	$
Total Profit / Loss	$	$	$

NOTES:

INVESTMENT PROPERTY ANALYSIS FORM

Property Address	Parker Duplex(Randall)		No. of Units	2
Purchase Cost	$ 120,000.00			
Down Payment	$ 24,000.00			
Closing Costs	$ 3,600.00			
Total Investment	$ 27,600.00			
	TERM	AMOUNT	RATE	P & I
FINANCING 1st Mortgage	20	$ 96,000.00	6.5%	$ 715.75
FINANCING 2nd Mortgage	10		7.5%	$ -
Depreciation				Year 1
Land Value		0.00%	$ 22,600.00	$ 22,600.00
Personal Property		20.00%	$ 2,000.00	$ 400.00
Building Value		3.48%	$ 94,400.00	$ 3,285
Land Improvement Value		5.00%	$ 1,000.00	$ 50.00
Total Depreciation			$ 120,000.00	$ 3,735
Annual Rent	850 per side	$ 20,400.00		
Less Vacancy Rate (10%)		$ 2,040.00		
Gross Operating Income		$ 18,360.00		
Annual Operating Expenses	AOI			
Real Estate Taxes	$ 2,997.00			
Maintenance	$ 1,800.00			
Insurance	$ 900.00			
Repairs	$ 100.00			
Management				
Plumbing				
Lawn and Snow	$ 200.00			
Utilities	$ 100.00			
Advertising	$ 50.00			
Supplies	$ 200.00			
TOTAL	$ 6,347.00			
I. Gross Operating Income GOI			$ 18,360.00	
minus	Operating Expenses OE		$ 6,347.00	
equals	Net Operating Income NOI		$ 12,013.00	
minus	Annual Debt Service ADS		$ 8,589.00	
equals	Cash Flow Before Taxes CFBT		$ 3,424.00	

Investment property analysis form (example)

(continued from opposite page)

II.	Annual Debt Service ADS		$	8,589.00		
	minus	Interest		$6,169.00		
	equals	Principal Reduction PR	$	2,420.00	$	(93,580.00)
III.	Net Operating Income NOI		$	12,013		
	minus	Interest	$	6,169		
	minus	Total Depreciation	$	3,735		
	equals	Taxable Income	$	2,109		
	times	Tax Bracket		30%		
	equals	Taxes Paid (TP)	$	633		
iv.	Cash Flow After Taxes CFAT	CFBT minus Taxable income	$	1,315		
	Appreciation Estimate (AE)			2.00%	$	2,400.00
V.	ROI with Appr. (CFBT+PR-TP+AE/cash inv.)			27.6%		
VI.	ROI without Appr. (CFBT+PR-TP/ cash inv.)			18.9%		
VII.	Capitalization Rate (NOI divided by purchase price)			10.0%		
VIII.	Cash on Cash (cash flow bef. taxes div.by cash inv)			12.4%		
IX.	Gross Rent Multiplier(sale price div. by annual rent)			5.9%		
X.	Debt Coverage Ratio (NOI div. by debt service)			1.4		
XI.	Operating Exp.Ratio (op.exp. div. by gross op.inc.)			34.6%		
XII.	BER = Break-Even Ratio			81.4%		
	Operating Expenses + Debt Service/Gross Operating Income = BER					

This form is designed to assist in estimating the first-year benefits of a real estate investment. It does not consider the effects of selling or exchanging the property in the future. This form is not a substitute for legal or tax advice. Anyone contemplating the purchase of a real estate investment should seek the services of competent legal and tax advisors.

Note: To get the "Interest" number for the gray area in Section II (Annual Debt Service), go to any amortization schedule and find the interest for the first year.

INVESTMENT PROPERTY ANALYSIS FORM

Property Address			No. of Units	
Purchase Cost				
Down Payment				
Closing Costs				
Total Investment	$			
	TERM	AMOUNT	RATE	P & I
FINANCING 1st Mortgage		$		
FINANCING 2nd Mortgage				
Depreciation				Year 1
Land Value				
Personal Property				
Building Value				
Land Improvement Value				
Total Depreciation			$	$
Annual Rent				
Less Vacancy Rate (10%)				
Gross Operating Income		$		
Annual Operating Expenses	*AOI*			
Real Estate Taxes				
Maintenance				
Insurance				
Repairs				
Management				
Plumbing				
Lawn and Snow				
Utilities				
Advertising				
Supplies				
TOTAL	$			

Gross Operating Income GOI		$
minus	Operating Expenses OE	$
equals	Net Operating Income NOI	$
minus	Annual Debt Service ADS	$
equals	Cash Flow Before Taxes CFBT	$

Investment property analysis form (blank)

(continued from preceding page)

II.	Annual Debt Service ADS		$	
	minus	Interest		
	equals	Principal Reduction PR	$	$
III.	Net Operating Income NOI		$	
	minus	Interest	$	
	minus	Total Depreciation	$	
	equals	Taxable Income	$	
	times	Tax Bracket		
	equals	Taxes Paid (TP)	$	
iv.	Cash Flow After Taxes CFAT	CFBT minus Taxable Income	$	
	Appreciation Estimate (AE)			$
V.	ROI with Appr. (CFBT+PR-TP+AE/cash inv.)			
VI.	ROI without Appr. (CFBT+PR-TP/ cash inv.)			
VII.	Capitalization Rate (NOI divided by purchase price)			
VIII.	Cash on Cash (cash flow bef. taxes div.by cash inv.)			
IX.	Gross Rent Multiplier (sale price div. by annual rent)			
X.	Debt Coverage Ratio (NOI div. by debt service)			
XI.	Operating Exp. Ratio (op.exp. div. by gross op.inc.)			
XII.	BER = Break-Even Ratio			
	Operating Expenses + Debt Service/Gross Operating Income = BER			

This form is designed to assist in estimating the first-year benefits of a real estate investment. It does not consider the effects of selling or exchanging the property in the future. This form is not a substitute for legal or tax advice. Anyone contemplating the purchase of a real estate investment should seek the services of competent legal and tax advisors.

Note: To get the "Interest" number for the gray area in Section II (Annual Debt Service), go to any amortization schedule and find the interest for the first year.

Cost Recovery – Depreciation

Cost recovery (depreciation) is the periodic allocation of the cost of qualified assets. When a taxpayer, or in some cases a lessee, purchases a qualified asset they can recover the acquisition cost of the asset through certain deductions set forth in the Internal Revenue Code. The method and length of recovery periods depends on the type of property purchased. Below are the cost recovery tables for the various types of property. These tables are rounded to two decimal points for simplicity. Check with your tax advisor for the actual percentages.

Recovery Percentages for Residential Rental Property (27.5 Years)

Recovery Year	Jan	Feb	March	April	May	June
1	3.48	3.18	2.88	2.58	2.27	1.97
2–27	3.64	3.64	3.64	3.64	3.64	3.64
28	1.88	2.27	2.57	2.87	3.18	3.48
29	0.00	0.00	0.00	0.00	0.00	0.00

Recovery Year	July	Aug	Sept	Oct	Nov	Dec
1	1.67	1.36	1.06	0.76	0.45	0.15
227	3.64	3.64	3.64	3.64	3.64	3.64
28	3.64	3.64	3.64	3.64	3.64	3.64
29	0.15	0.45	0.75	1.06	1.36	1.66

Recovery Percentages for Non-Residential Real Estate Property (39 Years

Recovery Year	Jan	Feb	March	April	May	June
1	2.46	2.24	2.03	1.82	1.60	1.39
2–38	2.56	2.56	2.56	2.56	2.56	2.56
39–40	Pro-rated					

Recovery Year	July	Aug	Sept	Oct	Nov	Dec
1	1.18	0.96	0.75	0.53	0.32	0.11
2–38	2.56	2.56	2.56	2.56	2.56	2.56
39–40	Pro-rated					

Cost Recovery – Depreciation

(continued from opposite page)

Recovery Percentages for 15-Year Land Improvements

Recovery Year	Percentage	Recovery Year	Percentage
1	5.00%	9	5.91%
2	9.50%	10	5.90%
3	8.55%	11	5.91%
4	7.70%	12	5.90%
5	6.93%	13	5.91%
6	6.23%	14	5.90%
7	5.90%	15	5.91%
8	5.90%	16	2.95%

Recovery Percentages for Five-Year Personal Property

Recovery Year	Percentage
1	20.00%
2	32.00%
3	19.20%
4	11.52%
5	11.52%
6	5.76%

SAMPLE LEASE AGREEMENT
THIS IS A LEGALLY BINDING DOCUMENT

IF NOT UNDERSTOOD, CONSULT AN ATTORNEY

Agreement of lease executed this ___ day of _______________ 20___ between ____ (Landlord), and ________________________________ (Tenant(s) whether one or more:

1. PREMISE: ______________________________ Street: Landlord hereby leases said premises to the Tenant in consideration of the following rent to be paid by the Tenant to the Landlord. The Tenant agrees to use and occupy said premises only as a residential premise, and not for any commercial purposes. Tenant furthermore agrees not to participate in or allow any illegal activity on or near the leased premises, and understands that the Landlord may terminate this lease if any illegal activity is found or discovered. No other persons may occupy the premises without written consent of the Landlord. Subletting and/or assignment of the lease without written consent of the Landlord is prohibited. A guest may be any temporary visitor for a period not to exceed seven (7) days. Any additional persons other than children occupying the premises shall entitle the Landlord to an additional amount of monthly rental in the amount of $50 per person, per month. (Not allowed)

2. RENT: The Tenant shall pay rent for said premises as follows ___ Estate for Years or ___ Month-to-Month:

   a. ESTATE FOR YEARS: For a term to commence on ______________________________ and end on ___________________________ unless sooner terminated as hereinafter provided, the Tenant paying rent to the Landlord at his/her office $_____________________ in monthly installments of $_____________________, with the first such monthly installment due and payable to the Landlord on the ____ day of the month with a like payment on the ____ day of each and every month thereafter for the entire term of this lease. This Lease Agreement shall automatically renew for successive one-month terms unless superseded by a new written lease agreement, or terminated by either party in writing at least 30 days before the expiration of the initial term or successive term.

b. MONTH-TO-MONTH: Tenant and Landlord agree that Tenant shall be a month-to-month tenant, and shall pay the Landlord a monthly rental amount of ____________________ dollars ($_____________), payable in advance on the ____ day of each and every month at the Landlord's office, the first such monthly rental payment being made herewith.

3. LATE CHARGE: If the rent is not received by the Landlord within three (3) days from the date it is due, the Tenant shall pay, in addition to the rental as herein above described, a late charge of $25.00, and in addition the sum of $5.00 for each and every day thereafter that the rent remains unpaid. Landlord and Tenant agree that the Landlord may accept and deposit a rental payment from the Tenant without said late charge, and that the same will not constitute a waiver of the Landlord's right to collect said late charge for the current month or serve to waive the Landlord's right to collect any future late charge in any future month.

Any check not honored by the Bank on which it is drawn will be considered by the Landlord and Tenant to be non- sufficient fund check and an additional fee in the amount of $40.00 plus any and all applicable late charges shall be immediately due and payable to the Landlord. If more than one non-sufficient fund check is received in a twelve-month period, all future payments will be made via cash, a cashier's check or money order.

4 SECURITY DEPOSIT: The Tenant has deposited, and the Landlord hereby acknowledges receipt of a security deposit in the sum of $_____________ for the faithful performance of all of the terms of this lease. In no event shall Tenant be entitled to apply such security deposit as rent due hereunder. In the event of Tenant's breach of or the termination of this lease, the Landlord may apply all or any portion of the security deposit to payment of rent and any other

costs, expenses and/or damages suffered by Landlord as a result of Tenant's noncompliance with this lease. Said security deposit shall not be kept in escrow or in a separate fund and shall not bear interest. Under no circumstances can said deposit be used or applied by the Tenant for the payment of rent.

It is understood between the parties hereto that the security deposit will not be returned to the tenant unless the following conditions have been met:

a. Tenant has occupied premises for the full term of the lease.
b. Tenant has given thirty (30) days' notice from the first day of the month of his or her intention to vacate the premises.
c. Tenant has not damaged the premises, its contents, or its yard.
d. Tenant has left the premises, including the yard, in a clean condition.
e. Tenant has returned all keys.

5. UTILITIES: The following utilities are to be paid by the party whose name appears opposite each utility as indicated:

Gas	Tenant
Water & Sewer	Tenant
Electric	Tenant
Telephone	Tenant

In the event Tenant is paying utilities, Tenant agrees to apply for utility services prior to moving into the property and to register utilities in his/her name by not later than the commencement date as set forth in paragraph 2.
Failure of the tenant to place utilities in his/her name by commencement date will cause this lease to be construed as never having taken place, and any monies paid to Landlord, as deposit or otherwise, will be forfeited by the Tenant to the Landlord. Tenant further agrees that trash removal service is for Tenant's personal use only and is not to be used for the disposal of hazardous materials or any furniture/ appliance.

6. LOCKS: Tenant acknowledges and receipts for one set of keys to the premises, and agrees to return the same number of keys to the Landlord upon the expiration of this lease. Tenant will not duplicate

any of the keys without notice to the Landlord. UNDER NO CIRCUMSTANCES will the Tenant be allowed to replace any lock of lockset without the express written consent of the Landlord. In the event any locks or locksets are changed by the Tenant, the Tenant hereby gives the Landlord permission to immediately, without notice, remove said unauthorized lock or lockset, and replace the same with a lock or lockset installed by the Landlord.

7. RULES AND REGULATIONS: The Tenant agrees for him/herself and his/her family, licensees, invitees and guests, to conform to the Rules and Regulations governing the premises and to any reasonable changes or new regulations that the Landlord may deem necessary.

8. ACCESS: The Landlord, or his or her agent, with one (1) day's notice to the Tenant, shall have free access at all reasonable hours to the premises for the purpose of examining, exhibiting or making repairs and/or alterations. The Landlord may have immediate access in the event of an emergency for the purpose of making repairs. In the event rightful access is denied to the Landlord, this lease, at the option of the Landlord, shall terminate, and the Landlord may take action accordingly.

9. ALTERATIONS: Tenant acknowledges that he/she shall make no alterations, decorations or improvements without the express written consent of the Landlord. In the event any of the foregoing is made, irrespective of the identity of that party making the same, the same shall become the exclusive property of the Landlord. The Tenant shall not make any holes in the wall, without repairing the same upon vacating.

10. EQUIPMENT: All appliances and equipment in the Premises may be used by Tenant, but only in a reasonable, safe, and non-destructive manner. In the event of temporary interruption, of electricity, water, gas telephone or trash removal service, or failure or breakdown of heating, air conditioning, kitchen appliances, plumbing or electric equipment, Landlord shall not be liable to tenant. Tenant shall notify Landlord of such interruption or failure, and Landlord shall make repairs with reasonable promptness and rent shall not abate during said periods.

11. TENANT DAMAGES: Tenant agrees that he/she is fully responsible for any breakage, damage, destruction, and/or soilage, which may be caused by Tenant or tenant's family, which occurs during Term of this lease or any extension or renewal Term. Tenant shall reimburse landlord as additional rent, for all expenses, damages, or costs incurred by Landlord by reason of said breakage, damage, destruction and/or soilage. Landlord shall have the option, but not the obligation, to cause repairs for which the tenant is responsible to be done at Tenant's expense

12. CONDITION OF THE PREMISES: The Tenant hereby acknowledges that he/she has examined the premises and that no representations as to the condition or states of repairs thereof have been made by anyone.
Tenant further acknowledges that the Landlord has promised no repairs, and the Landlord is not responsible for any repairs except those specifically written into this contract.
Tenant furthermore agrees to keep the premises in good repair, and upon vacating the same, deliver the premises to the Landlord in the same good condition as when leased, normal wear and tear excluded.
Tenant acknowledges that all light bulbs and sink strainers are in place, and agrees that upon termination, all light bulbs and sink strainers will be in place and in working order.
Tenant agrees to regularly dispose of all garbage in a neat manner, encasing all garbage in appropriate garbage bags, and to follow all rules and regulations imposed by any governmental authority with respect to the disposal of garbage or refuse.

13. INDEMNIFICAITON: Tenant agrees to indemnify and hold Landlord harmless from any and all claims, actions, damages, liabilities and expenses for any loss of life, personal injury or damage to property arising from any act or omission of the Tenant, his/her family, employees, occupants, servants, guests, invitees, or pets.

14. ABANDONMENT: The parties agree that any of the following acts will constitute common-law abandonment, and entitle the Landlord to take immediate possession or take steps to commence an eviction action:

a. Absence from the dwelling unit for seven (7) days without notification in writing to the landlord.
b. Termination of any utility service.
c. The establishment of another residence.

15. PHONE: Tenant agrees to keep Landlord informed of his/her phone number at all times.

16. DEFAULT IN RENT: In the event any rent is not paid when due, Landlord may terminate this lease after three days' written notice and take action for possession as provided by State law.

17. DEFAULT OTHER THAN RENT: If the Tenant shall default in fulfilling any of the terms, conditions or covenants of this lease agreement, other than the covenant for the payment of rent, the Landlord may terminate this lease be delivering a written notice to the Tenant specifying the breach and stating that the rental agreement will terminate 30 days after receipt of the notice if the breach is not remedied in 14 days. If substantially the same act(s) or omissions(s) occur within six (6) months, the Landlord may terminate the lease upon fourteen (14) days' notice specifying the breach and the day of termination. If this lease is month-to-month, nothing herein contained shall prevent the Landlord from terminating the tenancy at any time upon written notice being given to the Tenant at least thirty (30) days before the rental due date by which the Tenant must vacate the premises

18. PETS: The following applies to this lease:
No pets under any circumstances even for a visit.__________
Dog(s) allowed: Deposit to be______________________
Cat(s) allowed: Deposit to be ______________________
Other: ____

19. NOTICES: All notice to the Tenant shall be mailed or delivered to the Tenant at the address of the premises. All notices to the Landlord shall be made only to the following address or at such other address the Landlord may furnish to the Tenant.

20. INSURANCE: Tenant acknowledges that there is no security system at above-named property. LANDLORD STRONGLY RECOMMENDS THAT TENANT OBTAIN INSURANCE TO PROTECT SELF AND PROPERTY FROM LOSS that may occur from theft, vandalism, fire, water, water leaks or seepage from any source, rainstorms, smoke, explosions, sonic booms or other any other unforeseen damages that may occur. Landlord shall not be liable for any damage or losses to persons or property caused by acts or omissions of other tenants or other persons; tenant accepts all risks of loss or damage and agrees to hold Landlord harmless therefrom.

21. JOINT LIABILITY: In the event that this instrument is executed on behalf of the Tenant by more than one person, the liability of all persons so signing shall be joint and several.

22. SMOKE DETECTORS: Tenant has inspected the smoke detector(s) and agrees that they are operating properly. Tenant will ensure that detector(s) are tested monthly and batteries are changed as necessary.

23. OTHER CONDITIONS: No waterbeds allowed. Tenant responsible for snow removal of driveway and sidewalks. Tenant responsible for lawn care.

IN WITNESS WHEREOF, the Landlord and the Tenant(s) have executed this rental agreement on the date above first written. By signing this Agreement, the Tenant states that he/she has read this lease and understands the same. This is a legal and binding contract. Please read carefully before signing.

LANDLORD____

TENANT(S)____

____

Address____

City__________________State_____________Zip_________

2020 Real Estate Business Plan for Mr. Smart Investor

Especially Prepared for Jim Slick, Vice President of We Want Your Business Bank

BUSINESS GOALS

Mission
Our mission is to create income by purchasing undervalued properties to remodel and sell or retain as a long-term investment.

Mr. Smart Investor has over 7 years of experience as an investor and is a Mortgage Broker with Last Chance Mortgage. He currently has a rental portfolio of ten single homes, five duplexes and one fiveplex.

Profit will be generated by:
(1) Performing cosmetic improvements to single-family homes and selling them to generate 40–50% profit.
(2) Maintaining long-term rentals that generate a minimum of 10% cash on cash return.

Short-Term Goals
We will create and uphold a reputation in our community for honesty in our business dealings, and we will aim to achieve win-win results. We will focus on acquiring distressed properties that can be fixed and either sell them or use them as rentals.

During 2020we will purchase five properties to flip and five properties to rent. This will be the beginning of our long-term investment strategy to accumulate income-producing properties.

Actual number of properties purchased in 2018:
flipped: 3 sold: 2 rentals: 3

Long-Term Goals
Our objective in 2020 and each year thereafter until 2025 will be to purchase an average of five properties per year to fix and sell and five properties per year to increase our rental portfolio.

Pursuing this strategy over a five-year period will add 30 properties to our portfolio (single-family dwellings and duplexes) to go along with the 25 units currently in our portfolio (mix of single-family dwellings and multi units, each returning an average of $3,000 positive annual cash flow for a total income of $75,000 per year and annual asset appreciation of 3%.

Also during this five-year period, it is our objective that more than 30 properties will be sold for an average of $15,000 profit each, for a total of more than $450,000 cash income.

Ownership
Want To Be Wealthy LLC
We intend to be highly leveraged. All renovations will be done by licensed contractors.

DEVELOPING KNOWLEDGE OF THE MARKETPLACE

Target Neighborhoods
We will operate in the Midtown, Benson, and Northeast and Southeast part of the Omaha Metro area. These areas were chosen because properties can be purchased in the price range of $50,000 to $60,000 and because of our significant knowledge of the area.

Selecting Properties
We have developed a strategy involving purchases in the $50,000 to $60,000 price range. This price represents the lower end of what properties are selling for in the area, at least 20 to 40% less than average.

1. $30,000 between our purchase price and typical sales price is necessary to achieve our profit margin of approximately $15,000.
2. For our rental portfolio a purchase price of at least 20–40% price differential from market value is necessary for each purchase.

In order to appeal to homeowners and renters, these properties should be 3-bedrooms for resale and a minimum of 2-bedrooms for rentals. Properties should be located close to schools and shopping and should include amenities that will attract young families and first-time buyers.

Locating Flexible/Distressed Sellers
Our target market will be sellers who are highly motivated and may be having financial difficulties, or those whose properties have been on the market for at least 3–4 months.

Properties that initially will meet our criteria include:
1. Foreclosures
2. Properties in disrepair
3. Property management problems
4. Estate sales
5. Absentee ownership
6. Tenant problems
7. Retirement or relocation

It is anticipated that these sellers will be willing to negotiate to meet our minimum criteria for purchases.

Developing a Network
To be successful with our strategy, we will establish strong partnership with other agents, banks, and others.

BUSINESS OPERATIONS

Target Customer
Age group of 25–44 years.

1. Resale Properties

Our target buyer is a young, dual-income family. These buyers will have adequate to good credit but may lack significant cash reserves to use as a down payment or closing costs. Purchase price in the $100,000 to $120,000 price range.

Our approach to these buyers will be to utilize creative solutions to their cash shortage by utilizing programs such as FHA, VA and others.

2. Rentals

For our rental portfolio our target market for tenants will include students, young couples, single parents, and dual-income families.

The target rent will be $650 to $900 per month. These tenants would also serve as perfect candidates to purchase the property in the future.

Performing Market Analysis
The source we will use to determine the value of a property will be market analysis available through Multiple Listing Service and our own experience over the past seven years.

Financial Analysis
Each property to be purchased will be analyzed to determine the value of the property, appropriate purchase price, detailed estimated cost of potential renovation, acquisition costs, and potential sale price as well as anticipated profit.

Financial Arrangements
We have established relationships with the following banks:

> We Want Your Business Badly, Yes We Can, First Preference, Last Resort Banks

so we will know in advance of our ability to purchase properties that meet our criteria. As we will only purchase undervalued properties, after the renovations are completed we will seek permanent financing based on appraisal.

Renovation Process
We intend to purchase properties that are sold well below market value and will require minimal cosmetic updates and improvements. We anticipate that every property will require at least some cosmetic improvements to increase its value. It is our intent for these properties to be sold within a period of 90 to 120 days encompassing acquisition, remodeling, and purchase by buyer.

To perform these renovations as quickly and efficiently as possible we have assembled an experienced crew that we have used extensively over the past seven years. Additionally, we have sufficient experience and knowledge to determine the estimated costs and time frame required to complete a project. We anticipate that each project should be completed within 45 days from start to finish.

Based on our experience, the following improvements will significantly increase the value of each property:

1. Update kitchen: Install new cabinets if necessary, ceramic tile floor, new countertops, dishwasher and other appliances.

2. Replace carpet, refinish wood floors, install new blinds, etc.
3. Update bathroom fixtures including vanities, etc.
4. Paint interior/exterior as necessary.
5. Perform landscaping to improve exterior appearance.
6. Perform general overall polishing of property. We will keep in mind that our target sale price is in the $100,000 to $120,000 range.

Each property will be evaluated on its own merits, but the renovation costs are expected to range between $10,000 and $20,000. Properties that are purchased at $30,000 to $40,000 below market value will provide sufficient differential to achieve our desired return within 90–120 days from acquisition to sale.

Our renovation process model assumes that the six key tasks stated above represent the entire work to be completed. This assumption will be validated prior to purchase by means of a thorough inspection process. Our inspections will be done by licensed contractors, so there will no surprises regarding the renovation costs.

On occasion, however, a property may be available that may require a much higher remodeling price that would be justified by an opportunity to make a lot of money. These properties may require structural improvements or other major remodeling. These could be properties that are in terrible disrepair.

Another exception to our typical purchase criteria may be a small property that is surrounded by much larger and more expensive homes in a very desirable neighborhood. These scenarios do not meet our investment strategy but may be considered depending on the money needed to complete the project.

Selling Properties

After each property has been renovated it will be listed for sale. As our target consists of 25- to 44-year-olds who may only have enough of a down payment for an FHA mortgage, we expect to offer assistance with closing costs.

Rental Portfolio

Careful attention will be given during the purchase process to find potential rental properties that would meet the criteria for our long-term investment portfolio. In order for these properties to meet our standards they must pass the following performance measures:

1. We must be able to buy and fix the property with minimal cash outlay.
2. The property must be located in a desirable area (family-friendly neighborhood) to ensure better than average appreciation and better tenants, and it must be purchased at a price below market value.
3. The income and expense streams must be favorable to net a positive cash flow of at least $3,000 per year from each property.

Timeline

In summary, following the timeline identified throughout this document, we expect to purchase an average of one property per month

Managing our Properties

We are a very successful enterprise with over seven years of investment experience. We have an excellent system in place to continue to monitor our portfolio. We know every month how each property is performing. This is accomplished by our monthly profit and loss statement.

We are confident that our experience and success over the years merit strong consideration to obtain approval for a working line of credit in the amount of $100,000. Thank you very much for your consideration, and we look forward to establishing a mutually beneficial relationship.

GLOSSARY

Accumulated depreciation The total amount of depreciation expense that has been claimed by a property owner.

Acquisition cost The price and all fees required to obtain a property.

Acquisition loan Money borrowed to purchase a property.

Active investor An investor who manages his or her own properties rather than hiring a property management company to do it.

Adjusted cost basis The cost of any improvements made to a property.

Adjusted tax basis The original cost or other basis of a property, reduced by depreciation deductions and increased by capital expenditures.

Annual debt service (ADS) The total amount of principal and interest that must be paid each year to satisfy the obligations of a loan contract.

Assessed value A property's value for property tax purposes.

Averaging method Method of calculating next year's vacancy rate for a rental property by averaging previous years' vacancy rates.

Balloon loan A loan that has level monthly payments that will amortize it over a stated term (such as 30 years) but requires a lump sum payment of the entire principal balance at the end of a shorter term (for example, 10 years).

Balloon payment An installment payment that is much larger than the other scheduled payments. It is usually the last payment of a balloon loan.

Bird dog A person who finds properties for potential investors and receives a referral fee if the investor buys the property.

Bridge loan Mortgage financing between the termination of one loan and the beginning of another loan.

Building permit Permission granted by a local government or agency to build a specific structure at a specific site.

Break-even ratio (BER) This ratio measures the amount of money going out of an investment property against the amount of money coming in. The BER must be less than 100% for an investment to be viable. Lenders typically require a BER of 85% or less.

Buy and hold Investment strategy in which the investor purchases a residential property with the intention of holding it for several years and renting it to tenants.

Capital Money used to create income, either as an investment in a business or an income property.

Capital expenditure The cost of an improvement made to extend the useful life of a property or to raise its value, such as adding a room. The cost of repairing a property is not a capital expenditure. Capital expenditures are appreciated over their useful life, but repairs are subtracted from income for the current year.

Capital improvement Any structure or component erected as a permanent improvement to real property that increases the property's value and/or extends its useful life.

Capitalization (Cap) rate The ratio of the net operating income of a property to the proposed asking price. This figure is used to estimate the potential return on a real estate investment.

Carrying charges Expenses necessary for holding property, such as taxes and interest on idle property or property under construction.

Cash flow before taxes (CFBT): Net operating income from an investment property, minus debt service and capital expenditures, plus loan proceeds (if any) and interest earned (if any). CFBT represents the annual cash flow available before income tax deductions are considered.

Cash flow after taxes (CFAT) Cash generated from a property after taxes have been taken into account. This figure is calculated by subtracting the tax liability from cash flow before taxes.

Cash on cash return (COC) Ratio used to evaluate the long-term performance of a real estate investment. To obtain the COC, divide the property's annual cash flow (usually the first year before taxes) by the amount of the initial capital investment (down payment, loan fees, and acquisition costs).

Cash out Cash given to the borrower from the proceeds of a loan.

Cash-out refinance A refinance transaction in which the new loan amount exceeds the total of the principal balance of the existing first mortgage and any secondary mortgages or liens, together with closing costs and points for the new loan. This excess is usually given to the borrower in cash.

Collateral Property pledged as security for a debt.

Common area maintenance (CAM) Charges paid by the tenant of a commercial property for the upkeep of areas designated for use and benefit of all tenants. CAM charges are common in shopping centers, where tenants are charged for parking lot maintenance, snow removal, and utilities.

Contractor A person who contracts to provide specific goods or services.

Creative financing Any financing arrangement other than a traditional mortgage from a third-party lending institution.

Credit line A loan that allows revolving use of the credit; that is, after funds have been borrowed and repaid they may be borrowed again without applying for a new loan.

Debt coverage ratio (also known as debt service coverage ratio) (DCR) A ratio used in underwriting loans for income-producing property. To calculate DCR, divide the property's net operating income by its total annual debt service. Lenders typically require a DCR of 1.2 or more.

Deferred maintenance Physical depreciation of a property due to lack of normal upkeep.

Depreciation A method of allocating the cost of a tangible asset over its useful life. Businesses depreciate long-term assets for both tax and accounting purposes.

Double net lease (NN) Lease in which the tenant agrees to pay a basic monthly rent as well as property taxes and property insurance, and the property owner is responsible for paying all other operating expenses.

Down payment An initial amount paid on a property at the time of purchase.

Due diligence The act of carefully reviewing, checking, and verifying all of the facts and issues involved in a transaction before proceeding.

Federal Fair Housing Law A federal law that forbids discrimination on the basis of race, color, sex, religion, or national origin in the selling or renting of property.

Flipping Buying a property, improving it, and reselling it for a profit.

Gross operating income (GOI) The scheduled income for a rental property, less vacancy and credit loss, plus income from other sources such as coin-operated laundry equipment, vending machines, and garage rentals.

Gross rent multiplier (GRM) The purchase price of a property divided by its annual rental income before expenses such as property taxes, insurance, utilities, and maintenance.

Gross scheduled income The total annual income that would be produced if every unit in a rental property was rented and rent was collected from every tenant.

Highest and best use The use that is most likely to produce the greatest net return to the land and/or building over a given period.

Holdover tenant A tenant who remains in possession of leased property after the expiration of the lease term.

Housing code Local government ordinance that sets minimum standards of safety and sanitation for existing residential buildings.

Improvements Additions to raw land (such as buildings, streets, and sewers) that increase the value of the property.

Interim financing A loan, including a construction loan, that is used when the property owner is unable or unwilling to arrange permanent financing.

Internal rate of return (IRR) Rate of return on investment capital each year it remains in the investment. To compute IRR, divide the annual cash flow (return on investment) by the purchase price of the property.

Lease A contract in which, in exchange for a rent payment, the owner of a real property transfers the rights of possession to a tenant for a specified period of time (the term of the lease).

Lease option A lease combined with an option agreement that gives the tenant the right to purchase the property under specified conditions.

Lease purchase A lease combined with a purchase agreement that obligates the tenant to purchase the property under specified conditions.

Lessee (Tenant) A person to whom property is rented under a lease.

Lessor (Landlord) One who rents property to another under a lease.

Letter of intent Written expression of desire to enter into a contract without actually doing so.

Lien A claim on a property of another as security for money owed. Liens may include legal judgments, mechanics' liens, mortgages, and unpaid taxes.

Like-kind property Property having the same nature as another property.

Limited partnership Business arrangement in which at least one partner is passive and limits liability to the amount invested and at least one partner has liability beyond the monetary investment.

Line of credit An agreement by a lender to extend credit up to a certain amount for a certain time without the need for the borrower to file another application.

Loan to value Ratio of the loan amount to the appraised value of a property. A higher LTV means greater leverage for the investor and higher financial risk for the lender. A lower LTV means less leverage for the investor and lower financial risk for the lender.

Net cash flow Income produced by an investment property after subtracting expenses such as principal, interest, taxes, and insurance.

Net operating income (NOI) The total income an investment property generates after expenses (not including debt service).

No cash out refinance Refinance in which the amount of the new mortgage covers the remaining balance of the first loan, closing costs, any liens and cash no more than 1% of the principal on the new loan.

Non-disclosure non-compete (NDNC) Term used in commercial and multi-unit property listings. Sellers can require potential buyers to sign a NDNC prior to showing them the property's financials or scheduling an on-site visit.

Operating expense (OE) The total cost associated with operating a rental property, not including debt service, income taxes, or depreciation.

Operating expense ratio (OER) The ratio of a property's total operating expenses to its gross operating income (GOI). OER is useful for comparing the expenses of similar properties.

Option The right to purchase or lease a property upon specified terms within a specified period of time.

Ordinances Municipal rules governing the use of land.

Owner financing (also known as seller financing) A financing method in which a buyer borrows from and makes payments to the seller instead of a bank. Sometimes the buyer takes over the seller's payments. Owner financing can be done when a buyer cannot qualify for a bank loan for the full purchase price.

Passive investor A real estate investor who pays a property management company to handle day-to-day maintenance, repairs, rent collection, and other responsibilities.

Pro forma A presentation of data, such as a balance of income statement, in which certain amounts are hypothetical. For example, a pro forma balance sheet might show a debt issue that has been proposed but has not been consummated.

Raw land See Unimproved property

Real estate investment Non-owner-occupied real property.

Real estate investor A person who buys real estate for investment purposes rather than for their primary residence.

Refinance Process in which a borrower pays off one loan with the proceeds from another.

Regression The idea that the value of a better-quality property is adversely affected by the proximity of a lesser-quality property.

Regulation Z Federal regulation requiring creditors to provide full disclosure of the terms of a loan.

REO Property that has been reclaimed by a bank or government agency after the foreclosed property failed to sell at a real estate auction.

Residual Value or income remaining after deducting an amount necessary to meet fixed obligations.

Return on investment (ROI) with appreciation This figure takes into account the four benefits of investing in real estate: income, principal reduction, appreciation, and depreciation. It shows how the potential investment compares against other properties that are under consideration.

Return on investment (ROI) without appreciation This figure takes into account three of the four benefits of investing in real estate: income, principal reduction, and depreciation. It shows how the potential investment compares against other properties that are under consideration.

Section 1031 Section of the Internal Revenue Code dealing with tax-free exchanges of like-kind property.

Section 8 Privately owned rental dwelling units participating in the low-income rental assistance program created by 1974 amendments to Section 8 of the 1937 Housing Act.

Security deposit Cash payment required by landlord to be held during the term of the lease to offset damages incurred due to actions of the tenant.

Seller financing. See Owner financing

Single net or "N" lease Lease in which the tenant pays the basic monthly rent plus property taxes, and the property owner pays operating expenses (common area maintenance, or CAM) and property insurance.

Taxable income or loss Net operating income from an investment property, minus interest, depreciation, and loan costs, plus interest earned on property bank accounts.

Time is of the essence A phrase that, when inserted in a contract, requires that all references to specific dates and times of day noted in the contract be interpreted exactly as stated.

Triple net lease Lease in which the tenant pays a basic monthly rent as well as property taxes, property insurance, and maintenance expenses.

Unimproved property Land that has received no development, construction, or site preparation (also known as raw land).

Unrealized gain Excess of current market value over cost for an asset that is not sold.

Unrecorded deed Instrument that transfers title from one party (grantor) to another party (grantee) without providing public notice of the change in ownership.

Vacancy and credit loss Income that is not generated by a rental property due to vacant units (vacancy) or non-payment of rent (credit loss).

Wholesale Purchasing a property with the intention of reselling it quickly at a higher price.

Wraparound mortgage Loan arrangement in which an existing loan is retained and an additional loan is made that equals or exceeds the existing loan.

Yield Measurement of the rate of earnings of an investment.